WH'd THE
STOPCOCK?

HELP! WHERE'S THE STOPCOCK?

A FIX-IT FOR EVERY HOME NIGHTMARE

DRINA VANNER

foulsham
LONDON • NEW YORK • TORONTO • SYDNEY

foulsham

The Publishing House, Bennetts Close, Cippenham, Berkshire, SL1 5AP, England

ISBN 0-572-02423-1

Whilst every effort has been made to ensure the accuracy of all the information contained within this book, neither the author nor the publisher can be liable for any errors. When carrying out any do-it-yourself job, always exercise great care over safety matters and **always** turn off electricity and water supplies at source before attempting any emergency repair. Contact a qualified electrician, plumber or builder if you are unsure in any way. Never attempt to repair gas faults yourself and telephone the emergency number listed in the telephone book if you smell gas.

Printed in Great Britain by Redwood Books, Trowbridge

Contents

INTRODUCTION

Ignorance can be expensive. How many times have you called out a plumber, a mechanic or a handyman only to be told that all that was required was that a nut needed to be tightened, a battery charged, or a fuse mended? And putting cost aside, if the car breaks down, the washing machine floods or the sink gets blocked, finding someone else to sort out the problem can lead to much time-wasting, inconvenience and stress.

The aim of this book is to help you to help yourself. In straightforward language and with clear step-by-step illustrations, I have aimed to demonstrate exactly how to tackle practical problems of all kinds, from electrical faults to stains, from frozen pipes to creaking stairs.

The book also serves as a simple DIY manual, offering tried-and-tested approaches to basic domestic challenges, such as wallpapering, painting, tiling and putting up shelves and cabinets. Additionally, I have included a section filled with useful tips about a range of common problems: houseplants dying, keys sticking in locks, plaster cracking, and even what to do with smelly wellies in the hall!

I do hope that this book is as useful for you as it has been enjoyable for me to write.

Drina Vanner

1

WATERWORKS

Your water supply

Turning off your mains supply

Water is pumped into your house under pressure from a mains supply. This mains supply can be turned off and on at a stopcock. It is essential that you know where this stopcock is, as you may need to turn it off quickly in an emergency. The most likely place to find it is under the kitchen sink. You may also want to turn off the water when doing repairs.

If you don't know where your stopcock is, find it now and label it clearly.

WE CAN TURN OFF THE MAINS WATER SUPPLY WITH THIS STOPCOCK

Emergency action – turning it all off

❶

Turn the boiler and immersion heater off.

❷

Turn all the cold water taps on.

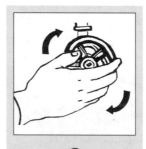

❸

Turn any known stop valves off. The most likely place to find your stopcock is under the sink.

❹

Phone the plumber.

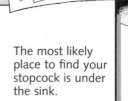

TRADE TIPS

The most likely place to find your stopcock is under the sink.

Turning off part of your supply

There are stop valves throughout your house which control the water supply to different rooms or appliances. This means that you can isolate and turn off just that part of your water supply. Make sure you know where these stop valves are and label them.

Finding your stop valves

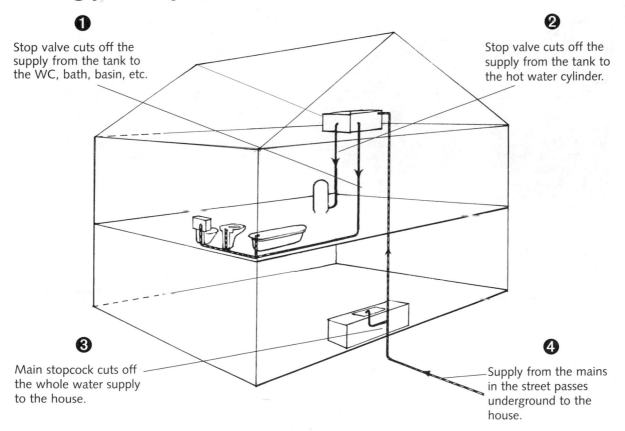

❶ Stop valve cuts off the supply from the tank to the WC, bath, basin, etc.

❷ Stop valve cuts off the supply from the tank to the hot water cylinder.

❸ Main stopcock cuts off the whole water supply to the house.

❹ Supply from the mains in the street passes underground to the house.

Water pipes

Burst pipes

If you have a burst pipe, you can make temporary repairs quite easily, to keep matters under control until the plumber comes.

Temporary repairs for burst pipes

Large hole

❶

Turn off the main stopcock. Cut a length of garden hose and make a slit down it. The hose must be long enough to cover the hole and extend at least 12 cm/5 in beyond the damage.

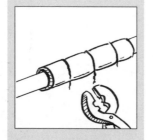

❷

Dry the affected pipe. Fit the hose over the area of the hole. Secure the hose by twisting loops of wire tightly around it, using pliers. Turn on the water supply.

Small hole

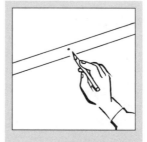

❶

Turn off the main stopcock. Insert a sharp pencil into the hole and snap off the lead. This will plug the hole.

❷

Thoroughly dry off the pipe, then apply plastic insulating tape to cover. Turn on the water supply.

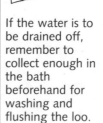

If the water is to be drained off, remember to collect enough in the bath beforehand for washing and flushing the loo.

Frozen pipes

If it is freezing outside and your taps suddenly stop working, it is very likely that the water inside them has frozen, causing a blockage.

Providing the pipe has not burst, there are several simple ways to deal with this problem.

Thawing frozen pipes

METHOD

 ❶

Turn on the affected tap. Using a hairdryer, blow hot air along the frozen pipe, starting from the end nearest the tap.

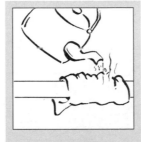

METHOD

 ❷

Wrap cloths or towels around the frozen pipes and pour boiling water over the material. Repeat as necessary.

METHOD

 ❸

Place a hot water bottle on the frozen part of the pipe.

FIRE RISK!

Never use a blowtorch or a naked flame to thaw pipes.

If the weather is likely to be very cold while you are away on holiday, keep the heating on very low to avoid pipes freezing.

Taps

Know your taps

There are several types of tap; their mechanisms work in different ways.
You must check what type of tap you have before you start any repair.

Types of tap

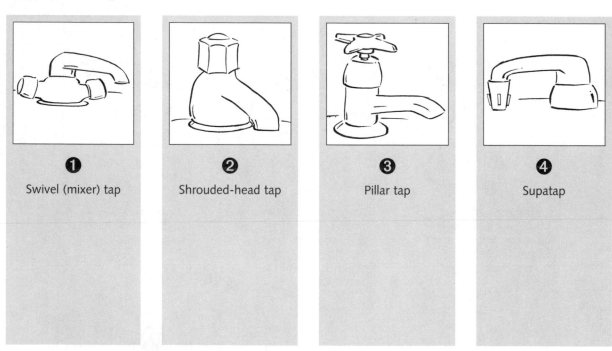

❶	❷	❸	❹
Swivel (mixer) tap	Shrouded-head tap	Pillar tap	Supatap

Replacing washers on taps

Dripping taps are irritating and will also cause unsightly stains. The most common cause of a dripping tap is a worn washer and replacing washers is very easy.

New washers can be bought at any hardware or DIY store – make sure you get the right size for your taps.

Replacing a washer on a swivel (mixer) tap

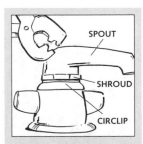

❶ Turn off both taps. It is not necessary to turn off the mains supply. Unscrew or lever up the shroud. Prise up the circlip by expan-ding it using a pair of pliers. Lift the spout from the mixer body. You may need to turn it to one side.

❷ Remove the worn washer and replace it with a new one that has been moistened with a little water. Reassemble the tap.

To avoid scratching the tap when unscrewing it, put a cloth between the jaws of the pliers and the tap.

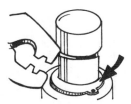

Replacing a washer on a supatap

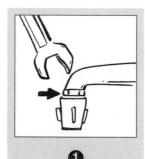

❶

Using a spanner, undo the nut at the top of the nozzle.

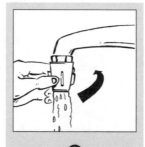

❷

Turn on the tap and keep turning to unscrew the nozzle. Do not panic! The increased water flow will reduce to a trickle just before the head comes off.

❸

Remove the nozzle and the water flow will stop completely.

TRADE TIPS

If you lose a valuable object down the plug hole, simply undo the U-bend under the plug hole to retrieve it (see page 25).

Replacing a washer on a supatap (continued)

❹

Remove the anti-splash device from the nozzle. To free it, push a pencil down into the top, or just tap the end on a hard surface.

❺

Prise out the washer-jumper from the anti-splash device.

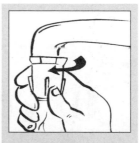

❻

Fit a new washer-jumper and reassemble the tap. Remember, the nozzle screws back the opposite way.

TRADE TIPS

To prevent losing screws down the plug hole whilst working on a basin or sink, put the plug in.

Replacing washers on pillar and shrouded-head taps

❶ Turn off the main water supply (see page 11).

❷ Open the tap fully and allow all the water to drain out.

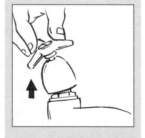

❸ Undo the screw in the top of the head and remove both the handle and the head cover. On shrouded-head taps, the screw is under the button on top of the head.

❹ Holding the body firmly with one hand, undo the large nut using a spanner. Lift out the head gear.

TRADE TIPS

To loosen a rusty screw, trickle vinegar on to the head and down the thread of the screw.

Replacing washers on pillar and shrouded-head taps (continued)

❺ Prise the jumper away from the head gear.

❻ Unscrew the nut that holds the washer to the jumper. Remove the washer and replace it with a new one.
If the nut is unmovable, buy a new washer-jumper complete from a DIY shop.

❼ Reassemble the tap and turn on the water supply.

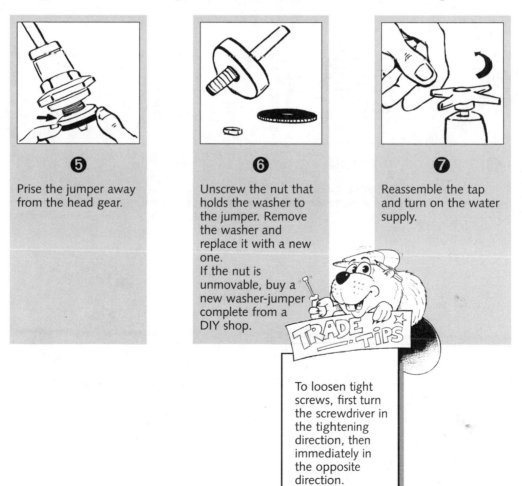

TRADE TIPS

To loosen tight screws, first turn the screwdriver in the tightening direction, then immediately in the opposite direction.

Washers on showers are called O-rings. These vary in size too, so make sure you buy the correct size for your mechanism.

Replacing O-rings on shower taps

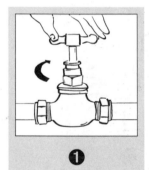

❶

Turn off the stopcock (see page10).

❷

Remove the flexible hose by unscrewing it.

❸

Undo and remove the screw on the diverter lever to expose the connector.

❹

Place a screwdriver in the slot of the connector and push to release and remove it.

Remove mildew from shower curtains by rubbing it with lemon juice, then soak the curtains overnight in salty water.

Replacing O-rings on shower taps (continued)

❺

Remove the mechanism by pulling it out of the tap body.

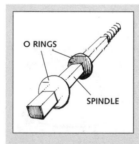

O RINGS

SPINDLE

❻

Slide the worn O-ring off the mechanism and replace it with a new one. Make sure you buy the right size!

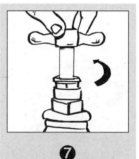

❼

Reassemble the tap. Replace the mechanism, connector and diverter lever. Screw back the flexible hose. Turn on the stopcock.

TRADE TIPS

To clear a blocked shower head, remove the head, poke through the holes with a needle, then soak the head in neat vinegar overnight.

Leaking tap heads

If a tap is leaking water from around the head, the spindle nut may be loose.

Tightening a leaking spindle nut

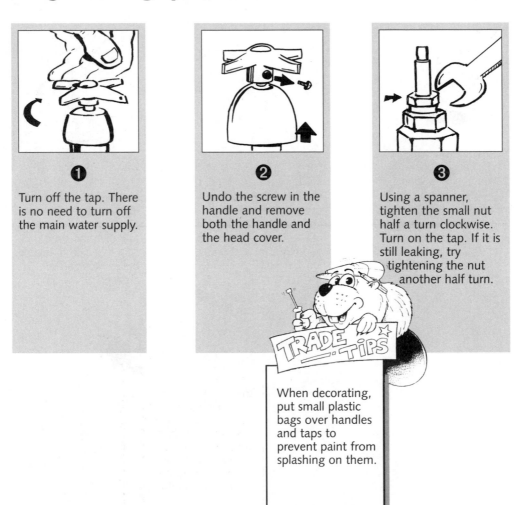

❶ Turn off the tap. There is no need to turn off the main water supply.

❷ Undo the screw in the handle and remove both the handle and the head cover.

❸ Using a spanner, tighten the small nut half a turn clockwise. Turn on the tap. If it is still leaking, try tightening the nut another half turn.

TRADE TIPS

When decorating, put small plastic bags over handles and taps to prevent paint from splashing on them.

If tightening the spindle does not stop the leak, then try repacking the spindle.

Repacking a leaking spindle

❶

Unscrew and remove the small gland nut, using a spanner..

❷

Remove the existing packing around the bottom of the spindle, then repack using new plumbers' string generously coated with Vaseline. Push it down using a screwdriver.

❸

Replace the gland nut and reassemble the tap.

Remove brown stains under taps by rubbing them with a mixture of salt and vinegar. Leave for five minutes, then rinse off.

Blockages

Blocked waste pipes

If your sink or basin won't empty, this is a clear sign that there is a blockage somewhere. Remember, however, that blocked wastepipes from washing machines, dishwashers, etc. may not be so obvious: the appliance may continue to run through its cycle but its performance will be affected. You should, therefore, check outside drains and gullies regularly to make sure these wastepipes are clear and running freely.

Unblocking sinks and basins

❶

Check the outside gully and clear out any debris that may be causing an obstruction.

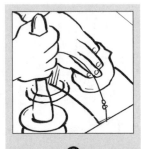

❷

Try using the plunger. First block up the overflow hole with a wet rag to prevent air escaping. Place the plunger over the plug hole and work the handle vigorously up and down.

❸

If the plunger does not work, try prodding, using a piece of curtain wire or a wire coat hanger, to dislodge the blockage.

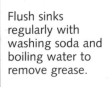

Flush sinks regularly with washing soda and boiling water to remove grease.

Blocked traps

All sanitary fittings have a trap in the waste pipe to prevent nasty gases and smells from travelling back into the house. They come in different types, but because of their shape they all become blocked rather easily. Fortunately, unblocking them is equally simple.

Unblocking traps

Screw plug trap

❶

Place a bucket under the trap. Unscrew the 'eye' at the bottom of the trap. Probe with a wire to dislodge the blockage.

Bottle trap

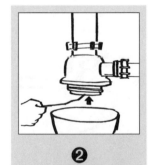

❷

Place a bucket under the trap. Unscrew the bottle at the base. Probe with wire, as before.

U-shaped trap

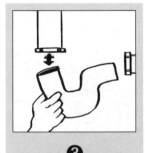

❸

Place a bucket under the trap. Unscrew both nuts and remove the U-bend. Probe with wire, as before.

TRADE TIPS

Wire coat hangers are useful for probing blocked pipes.

Blocked lavatories

Clearing blockages in lavatories is unpleasant but not difficult. If none of the methods below works, check to see if your outside drains are blocked (see page 27).

Clearing lavatories

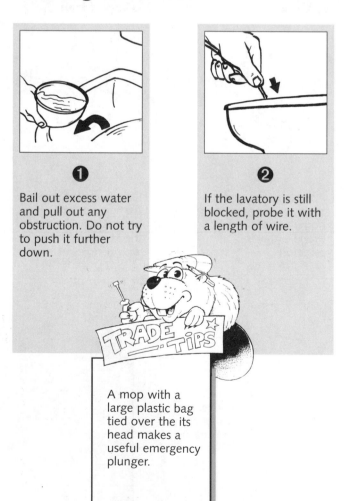

❶

Bail out excess water and pull out any obstruction. Do not try to push it further down.

❷

If the lavatory is still blocked, probe it with a length of wire.

❸

If the blockage is not visible, pump the handle of the plunger several times using a quick, vigorous action to force the blockage around the bend. When clear, flush the lavatory to re-fill it.

TRADE TIPS

A mop with a large plastic bag tied over the its head makes a useful emergency plunger.

Blocked drains

If none of your sinks, wash-hand basins or lavatories is draining properly, you probably have blocked drains.

Finding blockages in drains

Remove the manhole cover nearest to the house (the one at the highest level).

If it is empty, the blockage is between the manhole and the house.

If it is full, the blockage is between this manhole and any of the other manholes leading out to the main sewer in the road.

To prevent drains from freezing, sprinkle salt down them at night.

Using drain rods

❶ Assemble the drain rods. Fix the corkscrew fitting on the screw end of one rod; screw on two more rods and lower into the flooded drain, pushing towards the empty drain.

❷ Continue screwing on as many rods as necessary to reach the blockage. Always twist the rods clockwise, or they will come apart from each other.

❸ Push the obstruction until it clears, then withdraw the rods.

❹ If pushing does not work, substitute a rubber plunger for the corkscrew and use a pumping action to expel the blockage.

❺ Hose down or flush the lavatories until clean water runs through the manhole.

❻ Replace the manhole covers.

TRADE TIPS

If your drain covers are slimy and dirty throw them on to the garden fire to burn off grime.

Airlocks

Airlocks in pipes

Air trapped in water pipes will cause taps to hiss and splutter. These airlocks may even stop the flow of water completely, but they are usually easy to clear. You can use this method for any tap in the house that is giving trouble, always connecting it with the mains-fed kitchen tap.

Clearing an airlocked pipe – method 1

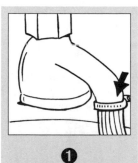

1

Connect a length of garden hose from the offending tap to the kitchen mains-fed cold tap. Secure well with jubilee clips.

2

Turn on both taps and allow them to run for several minutes. The pressure from the mains-fed tap should blow the air out. Leave both taps on until the gurgling noises stop completely.

A dulled steel sink can be cleaned by rubbing it with a little turps. Rinse and polish it with a dry cloth.

Clearing an airlocked pipe – method 2

Cold water system	Turn off the main stopcock (see page 11).
Hot water system	Turn off only the stop valve near the immersion heater (see page 11).

❶ Turn off the water supply (see left).

❷ Fully turn on all the appropriate taps, i.e. the cold taps if the cold water system is affected; the hot taps if the hot water system is affected.

❸ Close each tap about two-thirds of the way.

❹ Turn on the water supply.

❺ Check each tap for an even flow.

❻ Starting with the tap nearest the stopcock, open each one to about half-way.

❼ Again, starting with the lowest tap, open each one further to about three-quarters of the way.

❽ Check each tap for an even flow.

❾ Again, starting with the lowest tap, close all the taps until just a trickle flows from each.

❿ Fully close all the taps.

Clean chrome taps with neat washing-up liquid, then shine with a dry cloth.

Before you start, turn each tap on fully, noting how many turns it takes. Then you will know how many turns are needed for each position.

Airlocks in radiators

Air trapped in radiators will cause gurgling noises but will also prevent the radiator from working to its fullest capacity. It may feel hot only at the bottom – the top, where the air is trapped, will remain cold.

'Bleeding' radiators to release the air is simple – all you need is a radiator key, available from any DIY store.

Bleeding airlocks in radiators

Insert a radiator key in the side of the radiator and turn it anti-clockwise to allow the air to escape. Tighten as soon as water begins to hiss out. Hold something under the valve to catch any drips.

Leaking radiators

Wipe the joint dry, then tighten the nut using an adjustable spanner.

Tape foil to the underside of radiator shelves (shiny side outwards) to reflect heat.

Overflows

Overflowing overflows

Your house has external overflow pipes leading from each of your water storage tanks and lavatory cisterns. If one of these starts dripping or pouring out water, you must check the tank or cistern concerned. It is probably due to a faulty ball float or valve washer, both quite simple to replace. Valve washers vary in size but you can buy a selection for less than £1.

Find the fault

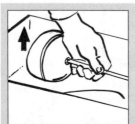

Lift the ball float arm in the tank that is overflowing – if the water shuts off completely the problem is a faulty ball float; if not, it's a faulty valve.

Faulty ball float

❶

To shut off the water supply until a new float is fitted, tie the float arm to a piece of wood placed across the top of the cistern.

❷

Unscrew the faulty ball float and replace it with a new plastic one. Untie the arm from the wood.

TRADE TIPS

To make a temporary ball float, encase the faulty ball float in a plastic bag, securely tied to seal it.

Don't let the water level in the cistern rise higher than 2.5 cm / 1 in below the overflow pipe.

Faulty valve

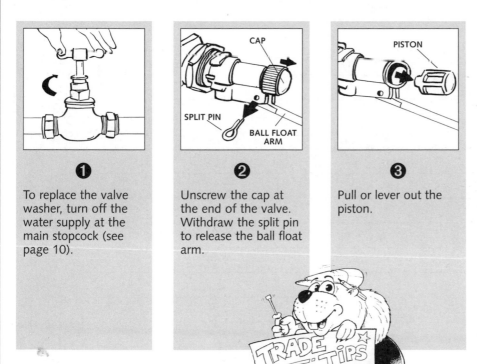

①
To replace the valve washer, turn off the water supply at the main stopcock (see page 10).

②
Unscrew the cap at the end of the valve. Withdraw the split pin to release the ball float arm.

③
Pull or lever out the piston.

④
Unscrew the piston, prise out the rubber washer and replace it with a new one. Grease the piston with Vaseline and replace it in the valve (washer-end first). Reassemble the whole and turn on the water supply.

TRADE TIPS

If the cistern water level is too high, either bend the float arm down (if not plastic) or adjust the nut near the ball valve to lower the arm.

Waterworks notes

2

ELECTRICITY

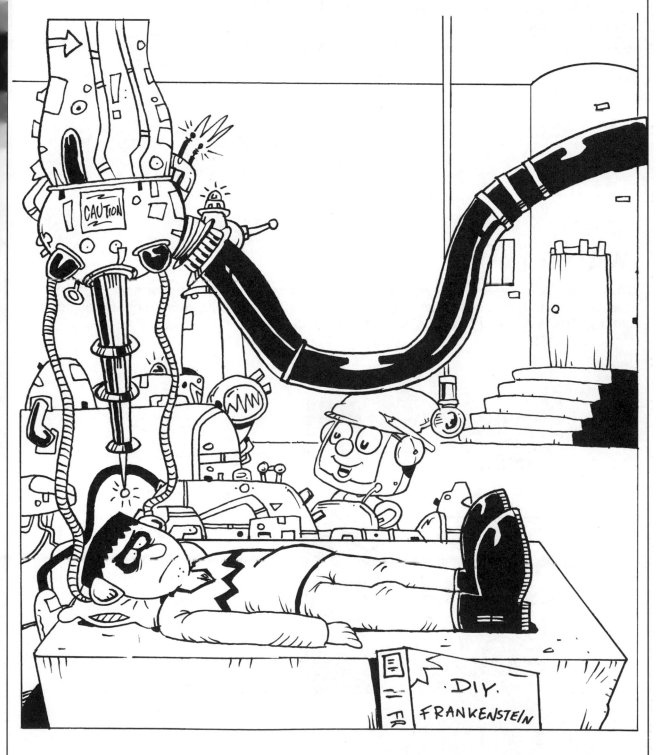

The fuse box

First find your fuse box

The fuse box controls the electricity supply into your house, by means of a mains switch, and also the distribution of power to all the rooms through individual circuits.

You have to know where the fuse box is so that you can replace blown fuses or turn off the mains power before you carry out electrical repairs.

Where do I look?

Your fuse box will almost certainly be positioned on an internal wall of your house but the exact location varies. Look under your stairs, in your hall and inside your broom cupboard. If your garage is attached to the house, it may be in there.

Fuse boxes old and new

There are several types of fuse box (see below) but they all work in much the same way. Each fuse covers one circuit – e.g. lights, immersion heater, etc, and if a fault occurs on this circuit, the fuse will blow.

Pre-war

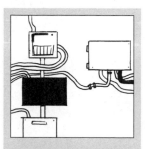

Lots of small boxes with individual mains switches. Wall sockets with round holes. If you've got one of these, have it replaced with a modern fuse board.

Cartridge

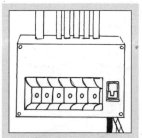

One mains switch. Fuse holders for lights, sockets, immersion heater, etc. When fuse is blown, replace fuse wire or cartridge (see pages 41–42).

Miniature circuit breakers

When a fuse is blown, a button pops out, identifying the faulty circuit. Once the fault has been found and corrected, simply push button in to reset.

When a fuse is blown, the trip switch moves automatically to 'off'. To reset, move the switch back to the 'on' position. But find the fault first!

Use the correct fuse

When you replace fuse cartridges or fuse wire, you must use the correct rating. On more modern boxes, colour-coded dots will tell you which cartridge to use.

White	5 amp	Lights
Blue	15 amp	Ring circuit (electrical sockets)
Yellow	20 amp	Immersion heater
Red	30 amp	Electric oven
Green	45 amp	Large double electric oven and hob

Keep a torch, fuse wire and spare fuses near the fuse box ready for emergencies.

Label your fuses

ALWAYS LABEL YOUR FUSES

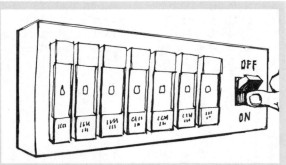

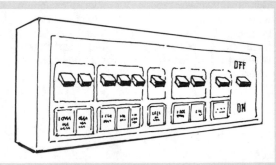

Whatever type of box you have, you should label all the fuses (e.g. lights, immersion heater) so that it is easy to find the correct one when you have a fault.

Some fuse box covers have spaces for this.

Labels on your fuse box will help you to identify which fuse holder belongs to which circuit.

The lighting circuit

Electricity enters your home through your electricity supplier's main cable which is connected to your fuse box.
Your fuse box then distributes it around your home.

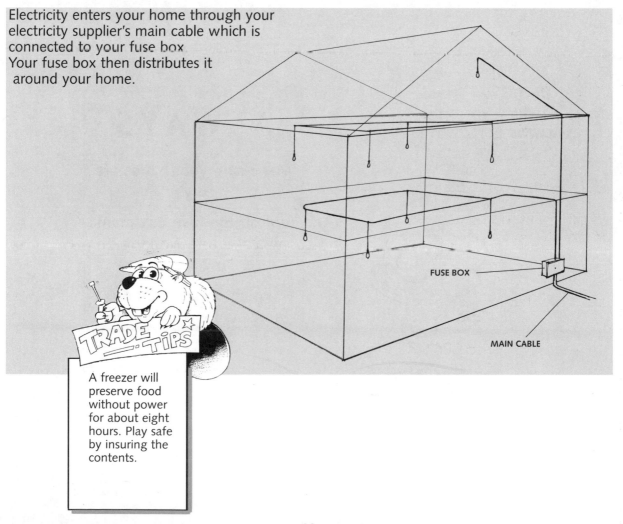

FUSE BOX

MAIN CABLE

TRADE TIPS

A freezer will preserve food without power for about eight hours. Play safe by insuring the contents.

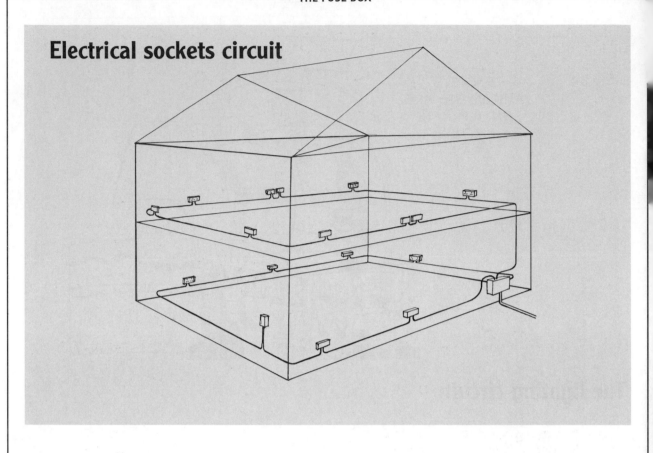

Electrical sockets circuit

TO AVOID ACCIDENTS, ALWAYS FOLLOW THIS ADVICE

ALWAYS

Make sure your hands are dry.

Turn off the fuse box mains switch before working on any fault.

Switch off and pull out plugs when working on appliances.

Fuses in your fuse box may blow for all sorts of reasons: because the circuit is overloaded, if the fuse wire is too low a rating, because of a faulty electrical appliance or just because the fuse is old. Replacing or rewiring fuses is not difficult, but if they blow repeatedly you should call in an electrician.

Replacing a cartridge fuse

❶
Switch off the mains power on the fuse box.

❷
Remove the blown fuse holder. If you have not identified and marked each fuse holder, you will have to find the faulty one by a process of elimination.

❸
Remove the faulty cartridge fuse and replace it with a new fuse of the correct rating. Replace the fuse holder. Switch on the mains power on the fuse box.

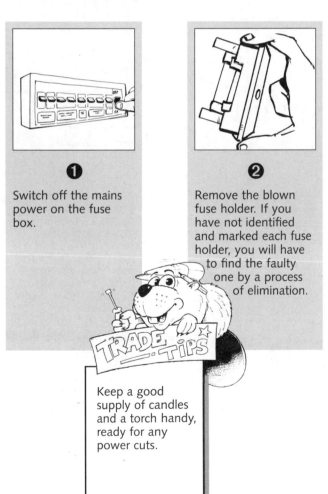

TRADE TIPS

Keep a good supply of candles and a torch handy, ready for any power cuts.

Rewiring a rewirable fuse

❶

Switch off the mains power supply on the fuse box.

❷

Remove the fuse holder. With rewirable fuses, scorch marks and the broken fuse wire will show you which fuse has blown. Remove the blown fuse wire.

❸

Cut a piece of new fuse wire of the correct current rating. Wind it round the screw at the top of the fuse holder. Guide the wire across the centre bridge and tighten round the lower screw. Replace the fuse holder and switch on the mains power at the fuse box.

If a fuse keeps blowing, call in an electrician.

Electrical plugs

Plugs on electrical appliances

If an electrical appliance suddenly stops working, it may well be that the fuse in the plug has blown. If it happens repeatedly, have the appliance checked for faults. NEVER be tempted to replace the fuse with one of a higher rating in the hope that it will last longer.

THERE GOES MY FUSE!

Replacing fuses in plugs

❶

Remove the plug cover by unscrewing the large screw in the centre of the plug.

E

N   L

❷

Pull out the cartridge fuse and replace it with a new one of the correct rating. Check that the wires are securely attached to the terminals. Refit the cover.

TRADE TIPS

Plug fuses are marked BS 1361.
Fuse box fuses are marked BS 1362.

Fuse ratings

Use 13-amp fuses for all high-power appliances, e.g. dishwashers, fridges, freezers, televisions, vacuum cleaners and washing machines. Use 3-amp fuses for all low-power appliances, e.g. electric blankets, clocks, lamps, hi-fis, etc.

You may need to change a plug because it has broken, or because you are attaching a new lead, or you may have simply opened it up to check that all the wires are securely attached. In every case, you must be sure that the plug is wired correctly.

The earth wire, which is coloured green and yellow, is always attached to the terminal at the top of the plug. For the other two wires, remember: **BL**ue wire (neutral) – **B**ottom **L**eft; **BR**own wire (live) – **B**ottom **R**ight.

ALWAYS ATTACH THE RIGHT WIRE TO THE CORRECT TERMINAL

Changing a plug

❶

Remove the cover and the fuse. Loosen the flex-retaining screws at the base of the plug and remove the flex. Insert the flex under the flex anchor strip in the new plug, then tighten the screws to secure.

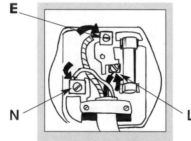

❷

Attach the wires to the appropriate terminals (see above) and tighten the screws firmly. Replace the fuse and screw on the plug cover.

Connecting a two-wire flex

If your flex has only two wires, connect the wires to the 'L' and 'N' terminals only as there is no earth wire to connect to attach to the 'E' terminal.

When re-using plugs, check that the fuse is of the correct rating for the appliance.

Flex

Types of flex

You can buy flex, or cable, by the metre from all hardware and DIY stores. It comes in several different types, each designed for a particular purpose.

PVC-coated three-core cable is the kind most commonly used for domestic appliances. PVC-coated two-core has only two wires and is used for appliances which do not require an earth, such as lamps and clocks.

Non-kinkable braided flex is good for irons and hairdryers.

Flex that is worn, cracked or badly kinked should be replaced.

Replacing a flex

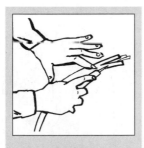

❶ Carefully cut about 4 cm/1 1/2 in down the PVC sheathing, using a sharp knife.

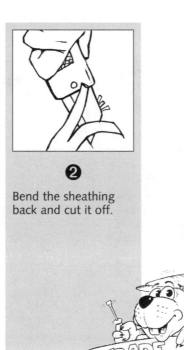

❷ Bend the sheathing back and cut it off.

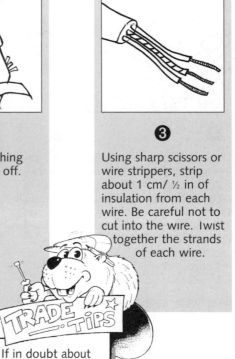

❸ Using sharp scissors or wire strippers, strip about 1 cm/ 1/2 in of insulation from each wire. Be careful not to cut into the wire. Twist together the strands of each wire.

If in doubt about which flex to buy, remember, the bigger the better.

Check the colours!

You may come across old flex that is colour-coded differently: red for live, black for neutral and green for the earth wire. Do not use this. If you find it on appliances, replace it with new flex.

Replacing a flex on an appliance (continued)

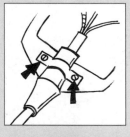

❹

Strip and prepare the ends of the new flex (see page 45). Undo the connector or casing of the appliance. Undo the screws holding the flex. Before removing, make a note of which wire goes to which terminal.

❺

Loosen each terminal holding the wires to remove the old flex. Remove any rubber sleeve or collar and transfer it to the new flex.

❻

To fit the new flex, connect the wires to the correct terminals. Slide the rubber sleeve back into position. Clamp down the flex over the sleeve by tightening the two screws. Reassemble the whole unit.

❼

Fit the plug (see page 44).

Regularly wipe the inside of your kettle with a damp cloth to prevent fur from forming.

Electrical sockets

Changing electrical sockets

Electrical sockets should be replaced if they are cracked or damaged in any way. You may also wish to change sockets to match a new decorative scheme. Note that the colour coding for the wires is different from that of electric plugs (see below).

Changing a socket plate

❶

Switch off the mains electricity at the fuse box.

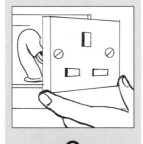

❷

To remove the socket plate, undo the screws and gently ease it off the wall box. A cable will be revealed, attached to the back of the plate. (If there are two cables, turn to page 48.)

(If there are two cables, turn to page 48.)

❸

Detach the wires from the terminals to release the plate. Reconnect them to a new socket plate. Screw the plate back on to the wall box.

❹

Switch on the mains electricity at the fuse box.

❺

COLOUR CODING

Wiring in electrical sockets is coded as follows:

Live (L) = red

Neutral (N) = black

Earth (E) = green

If a socket has become blackened or feels even a little warm during use, call an electrician.

Sockets with two cables

Sockets on a ring circuit have two cables inside, one bringing power in and the other feeding it to the next socket. Sockets with only one cable (see page 47) will have been added on as extensions to the original circuit.

Changing a socket plate with two cables

❶ Switch off the mains electricity at the fuse box.

❷ To remove the socket plate, undo the screws and gently ease it off the wall box. Two cables will be revealed, with their matching coloured wires twisted together and attached to the back of the plate.

❸ Detach the wires from the terminals to release the plate. Reconnect them to a new socket plate. Screw the plate back on to the wall box.

❹ Switch on the mains electricity at the fuse box.

TRADE TIPS

If a plug is cracked or damaged in any way, replace it immediately.

Dimmer switches

Replacing an ordinary light switch with a dimmer switch is very easy and gives more versatile, not to mention romantic, lighting.

Connecting a dimmer switch

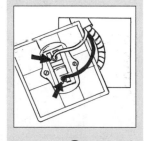

❶

Switch off the mains electricity at the fuse box.

❷

Double check that the power is not on, by turning on the light switch.

❸

Detach the switch plate by undoing the screws and gently easing it off the wall box. Make a note of which wire goes into which terminal.

❹

Disconnect the wires by unscrewing the terminals. DO NOT disturb the green earth wire attached to the wall box.

When removing a switch plate, cut round it first with a sharp knife to avoid damage to wallpaper.

Connecting a dimmer switch (continued)

One-way

⑤

Now connect your chosen dimmer switch. One-way switches have two wires – red and black. Connect these to the terminals of the new dimmer switch, following the instructions supplied. The red wire must be connected to the terminal marked 'com.'

Two-way

⑤

Two-way switches have three wires – red, yellow and blue. Connect these to the terminals of the new dinner switch, following the instructions supplied. Again, the red wire must be connected to the terminal marked 'com.'

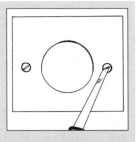

⑥

Screw the dimmer switch back on to the wall box. Switch on the mains electricity at the fuse box.

Keep old face plate screws when fixing a new plate. The new screws may have a different thread and so will not engage properly.

Lights

Faulty fluorescent lights

If your fluorescent light flickers and buzzes, or has blackened ends, the tube may need replacing. If it won't light at all, the starter is probably at fault.

Replacing a faulty tube

❶

Switch off the mains electricity at the fuse box.

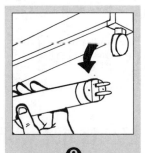

❷

Ease the tube out of one end of the hinged bracket, disconnecting the tube pins. Remove and replace with a tube of the same wattage.

Replacing a faulty starter

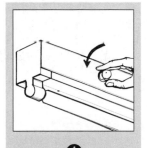

❶

Starters may be located at various places on the lamp fitting. To remove the starter, twist and turn it anti-clockwise. Insert a new starter, twisting it anti-clockwise into position.

❷

Switch on the mains electricity at the fuse box.

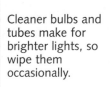

Cleaner bulbs and tubes make for brighter lights, so wipe them occasionally.

Christmas Lights

WHAT'S THAT ON TOP OF THE TREE?

IT'S A FLASHER UNIT

Be flash!

Turn ordinary lights into flashers by fitting a flasher unit (available at most DIY stores) into an empty bulb socket on your existing lights.

Lights not working?

1 Check that each bulb is pushed or firmly screwed into its socket.

2 Check the plug for loose wires or a blown fuse.

3 To find a faulty bulb, replace each one in turn with a working bulb.

TRADE TIPS

Always check that Christmas lights are working *before* you put them on the tree.

Electricity notes

3

ELECTRICAL APPLIANCES

Washing machines

Just calling out an engineer to look at your machine can cost anything up to £50 – and that's before he's laid a spanner on it. Fortunately, many faults are quite simple to put right yourself.

IF YOUR MACHINE'S NOT WORKING, CHECK THIS LIST OF FAULTS

FAULT	CHECK	ACTION
Will not start	● Machine is plugged in and switched on at the socket	Check the plug by fitting it into another socket. If it is faulty, see pages 43–4.
	● Door is securely closed ● Hoses are not kinked ● Water supply is on ● Fuses in plug and fuse box are OK	
Will not fill	● Hoses are not kinked ● Door is securely closed ● Water supply is on ● Inlet filters are not blocked	To check the inlet filter, turn off the water and unscrew the hoses to reveal the filters (see rear view on page 57).
Machine fills but the water empties from the drain hose	● Drain hose is at the correct height from the floor	See rear view (on page 57). Refer to the manual.
Door will not open	● Programme selector has been set to finish – and has finished ● You have waited two minutes if you have a safety latch ● Rinse hold button has not been selected (if applicable) ● If there is water in the drum	This may be because the lint filter is too full. Unscrew the filter slightly to release any excess water. Clean and replace the filter.
Soap dispenser drawer will not open or close completely	● That the drawer has been refitted correctly after cleaning	Remove and re-insert the drawer.

TRADE TIPS

White vinegar makes a good substitute for softener and is odourless.

FAULT	CHECK	ACTION
Suds overflowing	● Correct powder has been used ● Too much powder has not been used	To clear (most models): ● Switch off the machine ● Turn the programme selector to empty (at the end of the wash cycle) ● Switch the machine on ● See Tip below.
Water leaking out	● Hot and cold water hoses are firmly attached	See rear view below.
Machine stopped but full of water	● Drain hose is not kinked ● Whether rinse hold button is set ● Whether machine has 'paused' to heat water	See rear view below. Move the selector on to 'spin'. In an emergency, the water can be emptied by dropping the drain hose to floor level and allowing the water to drain out.
Clothes come out too wet	● That you have selected the right programme for the fabric	Select a different spin cycle.
Clothes remain dirty	● Correct amount of powder used ● Correct programme selected ● Machine not overloaded	

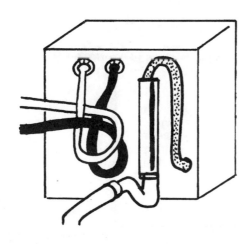

If your suds overflow, sprinkle salt or lemon juice into the soap powder compartment to disperse the bubbles.

Tumble dryers

Problems with tumble dryers tend to be more to do with the way they are loaded and set than with the machines themselves.

Check the filters and air vent frequently and keep them clear of fluff to reduce the risk of overheating or fire.

FAULT		CHECK	ACTION
Will not start	●	Machine is plugged in and switched on at the socket	Check the plug by fitting it into another socket. If it is faulty, see pages 43–4.
	●	Door is securely closed	
	●	Fuse is not blown in the plug or the fuse box	
Clothes very creased	●	Dryer is not overloaded	
	●	Correct heat setting has been selected	
Machine taking too long to dry and not drying well	●	Dryer is not overloaded	
	●	Correct drying time has been chosen	
	●	Correct heat setting has been selected	
	●	Filter is not blocked	Clean the filter regularly.
	●	Cold water inlet hose is connected to the cold tap and the water is turned on	

To help prevent clothes from freezing on the line in winter, put a handful of salt in the final rinsing water.

Dishwashers

Dishwashers are not complicated machines – minimise the risk of problems by cleaning the rotor spray nozzles and filters regularly and keeping the salt and rinse agent topped up.

FAULT	CHECK	ACTION
Will not start	● Machine is plugged in and switched on at the socket ● Water supply is on ● Door is securely closed ● Correct programme has been selected ● Hoses are not kinked ● Fuses are not blown in the plug or the fuse box	Check the plug by fitting it into another socket. If it is faulty, see pages 43–4.
Will not fill	● Hoses are not kinked ● Tap is turned on	
Machine fills but the water empties from the drain hose	● Drain hose is at the correct height above the floor.	See rear view (below). Refer to the manual.
Will not empty	● Drain hose is not kinked ● Waste filter is not blocked	See rear view (below).
Water leaking out	● Inlet and drain hoses are firmly attached to the machine	See rear view (below).
White deposits left on dishes	● You are using the correct salt	

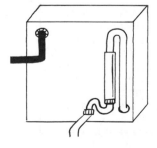

TRADE TIPS

Clean badly stained mugs, cups, etc. by rubbing with a damp cloth dipped in salt.

FAULT		CHECK	ACTION
Dishes still wet	●	Rinse aid dosage is not too low	Adjust the rinse aid setting.
Glasses still greasy	●	Rinse aid dosage is not too high	Adjust the rinse aid setting.
Stains left on glasses, cups, etc.	●	You are using the correct amount of detergent	Refer to the detergent packaging.
Glasses dull or misty	● ●	Rinse aid dosage is at the correct setting There is enough salt in the container	The rinse aid setting may be too low. Alter it.
Dishes remain dirty	●	Rotor spray arm nozzles are not blocked (see inside view below)	Remove the rotor arm by unscrewing the cap (see below) and wash it under a tap.
Machine emptying too slowly	●	Filter in the inlet hose is not blocked	See rear view (page 59).
Rattling noises during the wash	●	Dishes are stacked correctly	

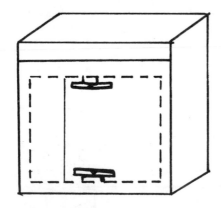

If a saucepan is badly burnt, sprinkle thickly with salt and leave overnight, then fill with water and bring to the boil. Finally, clean as normal.

Waste disposal units

Don't expect your waste disposal unit to chew up anything and everything. Dry and 'indigestible' items such as brown paper, string and plastic bags will certainly cause jams. Keep a release tool handy (see illustration) for when the going gets tough.

FAULT		CHECK	ACTION
Motor will not turn or reverse	●	Fuse has not blown in the control box or the main fuse box	Check the plug by fitting it into another socket. If it is faulty, see pages 43–4.
	●	Grinder jammed	Use the release tool – see below.
Burning smell	●	Coils have not burned out	Call an engineer.

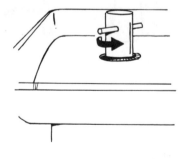

1. Switch off the power at the mains fuse box and the control box.

2. Fit the release tool through the sink outlet until it engages on to a nut.

3. Rotate the tool backwards and forwards to free the blockage.

4. Press the reset button.

5. Switch the power back on.

TRADE TIPS

Always run plenty of water through when using your waste disposal unit.

Kettles

Kettles, with their potentially lethal combination of boiling water and electricity, should be treated with respect. Never leave a boiling kettle unattended – even an automatic switch may fail, allowing the kettle to boil dry. If the flex becomes worn, replace it immediately.
If you live in a hard water area, descale your kettle regularly (you should not use artificially softened water for drinking).

FAULT	CHECK	ACTION
Water does not heat up	● Plug is working	Check the plug by fitting it into another socket. If it is faulty, see pages 43–4.
	● The flex is not faulty	See pages 45–6.
	● Element is not broken	Replace element (see below).
Flex coupler has ejected	● The kettle has not boiled dry	Push back the coupler when the kettle cools.
Slow at heating	● The kettle does not need descaling	Descale (see Tip below).

Replacing the element

❶

Hold the element inside the kettle with one hand and unscrew the shroud with the other hand.

❷

Pull out the element by twisting it gently and replace it with a new one.

NEVER BOIL AN EMPTY KETTLE

Descale a kettle by filling it with water plus 15 ml/1 tbsp of vinegar. Boil and leave overnight. Empty and rinse.

Toasters

With all the adjustable controls on today's toasters, burnt toast should be a thing of the past. But if your slice of bread is stuck and there's a cloud of smoke rising, don't forget to turn the plug off at the socket before you poke a knife in to investigate.

FAULT		CHECK	ACTION
No power or intermittent power	●	Plug is working	Check the plug by fitting it into another socket. If it is faulty, see pages 43–4.
	●	The flex is not faulty	See pages 45–6.
Toast burnt or not brown enough	●	Browning control is set correctly	Adjust control.
Toast not popping up	●	Mechanism not broken	Return appliance to the dealer.

Cleaning the crumb tray

Turn the toaster upside-down over a piece of newspaper. Remove the crumb tray, empty and wipe it clean, then replace the tray.

Fresh bread can be cut more easily if you warm the knife first in hot water.

Vacuum cleaners

Vacuum cleaners need regular maintenance to work properly. We all know about changing the bags, but filters need changing every few months too – check your manufacturer's handbook. Spare parts are readily available from electrical and hardware stores.

FAULT		CHECK	ACTION
Will not start	●	Plug is working	Check the plug by fitting it into another socket. If it is faulty, see pages 43–4.
Not picking up efficiently	● ● ●	Dust bag is not full Belt is not broken Brushes are not worn	Empty the dust bag. See below.
Smells of burning rubber	● ●	Belt is not loose String or cotton has not caught on the belt pulley	Fit a new belt (see below). Remove the obstruction.

Fitting a new belt

❶ Remove the front cover of the vacuum cleaner and pull the belt off the pulley, allowing it to drop down. Turn the machine on its side and remove the underneath cover.

❷ Lift out roller and belt and fit a new belt. Refit the roller and the underneath cover. Turn the machine upright, then stretch the belt clockwise back over the pulley. Replace the front cover.

If the belt is put on the wrong way, it will slip off when the motor is started. Remove and refit it the other way round.

TRADE TIPS

Clean dingy carpets by sprinkling salt over them, leaving it for a few hours, then vacuuming it up.

Irons

FAULT	CHECK	ACTION
No heat	● Plug is working ● The flex is not faulty	Check the plug by fitting it into another socket. If it is faulty, see pages 43–4. See pages 45–6.
Heats up but not to required temperature	● Thermostat is not faulty	Return to the shop or take for repair.
Steam spray is not working correctly	● Outlets are not blocked	Always use distilled water. Clear blocked steam vents with a descalant suitable for irons.

Covering an ironing board

The leg of an old pair of pyjamas makes an excellent ironing board cover. Slide the leg on to the ironing board and secure the ends with lines of running stitches.

When your iron is cold, rub the sole plate with methylated spirits to remove any stains.

Electric fires

Electric fires provide a good source of heat exactly when and where you need it. But they are also a common cause of house fires, so keep yours in good condition and remember to turn it off when you leave a room.

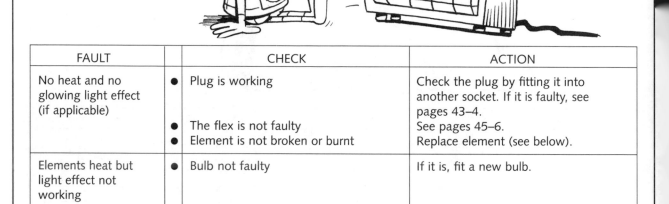

FAULT		CHECK	ACTION
No heat and no glowing light effect (if applicable)	●	Plug is working	Check the plug by fitting it into another socket. If it is faulty, see pages 43–4.
	●	The flex is not faulty	See pages 45–6.
	●	Element is not broken or burnt	Replace element (see below).
Elements heat but light effect not working	●	Bulb not faulty	If it is, fit a new bulb.

Fitting a new element

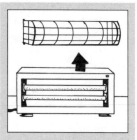

❶

Remove the plug from the socket. Release and remove the guard.

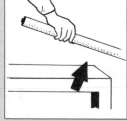

❷

Unscrew the nuts at each end of the faulty element.

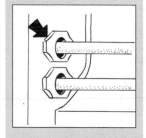

❸

Lift out and replace with a new element. Refit the guard.

Reflectors on electric heaters throw out most heat when they are clean. Shine them up every now and then with a silver polishing cloth.

Electrical appliances notes

4

WALLPAPER

Preparation

Preparation is the key to successful wallpapering. It may not be the most exciting part of the job but the results will be better in the long run. Take the time to measure carefully around the room and calculate exactly how much paper you need – use the chart below to help you. When working out the best place to start (see below), hold a roll of paper up to the walls so that you can see where the joins will fall and check the positioning of bold patterns.

	NUMBER OF ROLLS REQUIRED										
Measurement around room	9m / 30 ft	10.2 m / 34 ft	11.4 m / 38 ft	12.6 m / 42 ft	13.8 m / 46 ft	15 m / 50 ft	16.2 m / 54 ft	17.4 m / 58 ft	18.6 m / 62 ft	19.8 m / 66 ft	21 m / 70 ft
Height of room											
2.4 – 2.7 m / 8 ft – 9 ft	5	5	6	7	7	8	9	9	10	10	11
2.25 – 2.4 m / 7 ft 6 in – 8 ft	5	5	6	6	7	7	8	8	9	9	10
2.1 – 2.25 m / 7 ft – 7 ft 6 in	4	5	5	6	6	7	7	8	8	9	9

Where do I begin?

Ceilings

If a ceiling is to be papered, tackle it before the walls. Start at the window end.

Rooms without a fire-place

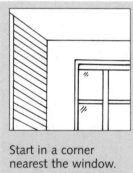

Start in a corner nearest the window.

Rooms with a fire-place

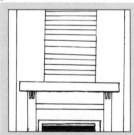

Hang the first length in the centre of the chimney breast. Work towards the door, first from one side and then the other.

Before you begin

Gather together all the tools and equipment you need. Large kitchen scissors can be used if you don't have shears and a picnic table will make a good pasting table. Stack furniture in the centre of the room and cover it with dust sheets. Remove curtains, etc.

TRADE TIPS

Always buy an extra roll of wallpaper. If you don't use it, you can usually return it.

Ceilings

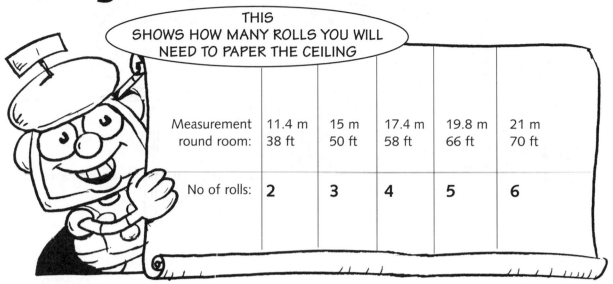

	11.4 m 38 ft	15 m 50 ft	17.4 m 58 ft	19.8 m 66 ft	21 m 70 ft
THIS SHOWS HOW MANY ROLLS YOU WILL NEED TO PAPER THE CEILING					
Measurement round room:	11.4 m 38 ft	15 m 50 ft	17.4 m 58 ft	19.8 m 66 ft	21 m 70 ft
No of rolls:	2	3	4	5	6

Where to start

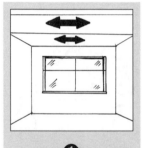

❶
Paper lengths should run parallel with the main window wall. Start at the end nearest to the window.

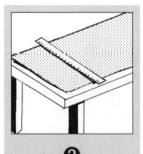

❷
To hang the first length, measure the width of the wallpaper and subtract 5 mm/ ⁄4 in to allow for overlap on to the wall.

Marking a guideline

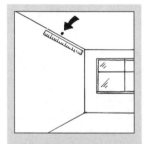

❶
Mark the measured width on the ceiling at each end of the wall.

❷
Pin a length of string from one mark to the other and draw a line.

TRADE TIPS

A wide paint brush can substitute for a paste brush.

Pasting and positioning the paper

❶ Measure and cut the number of lengths required, allowing 5 cm/2 in extra at each end for trimming.

❷ Paste and fold each length concertina style. (Always allow the paper to soak according to the manufacturer's instructions.)

❸ Drape the pasted length over a spare roll of paper – this makes it easier to hold and carry.

❹ Position the paper against the marked guideline and press it to the ceiling, holding the folded paper with the other hand. Keep folded paper close to the ceiling.

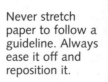

Never stretch paper to follow a guideline. Always ease it off and reposition it.

Hanging the paper

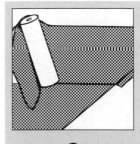

❶ Unfold the paper a fold at a time, brushing it into position until fully extended.

❷ Score the overlap at the wall ends, using the blunt edge of a pair of scissors.

❸ Trim 5 mm/ ¼ in outside the scored line so that the paper can turn slightly on to the wall below.

❹ Hang the next length, aligning it exactly with the edge of the first length. Seams must butt together, not overlap.

TRADE TIPS

Pour any leftover paste into a screw-top jar and keep it for sticking down loose seams, etc.

TIE A KNOT IN A CEILING LIGHT FLEX TO MAKE IT EASIER TO PULL THROUGH THE PAPER

Papering around light fittings

❶

Brush the pasted length towards the ceiling light in the usual way.

❷

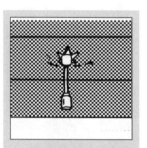

Cut a star shape through the paper where you judge the centre of the ceiling rose to be.

❸

Pull the flex through, then continue to hang the rest of the paper firmly on to the ceiling.

❹

Score and trim neatly around the rose plate, allowing 5 mm/ ¼ in to be tucked behind the plate if it can be unscrewed (remember to turn off the electricity first). Smooth the paper into place and tighten screws if necessary.

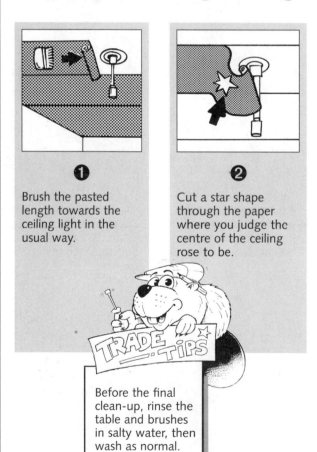

TRADE TIPS

Before the final clean-up, rinse the table and brushes in salty water, then wash as normal.

Walls

Preparing the walls

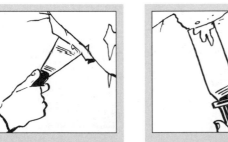

❶

ORDINARY PAPER
Soak the surface with hot water and washing-up liquid. Leave for 10 minutes and then scrape it off with a wide stripping knife.

WASHABLE PAPER
Hire a steam stripper from a DIY store. This saves time and energy.

❷

Fill in any cracks or holes with filler and a filling knife. When completely dry, rub down with sandpaper until smooth.

Cutting the paper

❶

Using a plumb line, draw a vertical line just less than one paper width away from the starting corner (which allows an overlap of paper to turn back and around the corner).

❷

PLAIN PAPER
Measure the height of the wall and add an extra 10 cm/4 in for trimming. Use this measurement as a guide for subsequent lengths.

PATTERNED PAPER
Match up the pattern of each piece with the previous one before you cut off a length.

TRADE TIPS

A plumb line is a string with a weight on one end. Hold it up against a wall, with the weight hanging down, to give a perfect vertical line.

THE HEAVIER THE PAPER, THE THICKER THE PASTE NEEDS TO BE

Pasting the paper

❶

Mix the paste in a clean bucket according to the manufacturer's instructions.

❷

Lay the first length face down on the table. Apply paste evenly, working outwards towards the edges.

❸

Fold the pasted ends into the centre, making one fold longer to remind you which end is the top. Allow the paper to absorb the paste for a few minutes.

❹

Carry the folded length over your arm.

TRADE TIPS

To keep a paste bucket clean, line the bucket with a clean plastic bag secured with tape. When finished, throw the bag away.

Hanging the paper

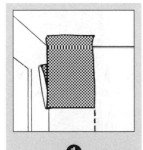

❶ Unfold the top end of the paper and position the length on the wall with its edge following the vertical line you marked. Leave 5 cm/ 2 in extra at the top, to be trimmed off.

❷ Smooth the paper using a paper hanging brush, working upwards, then sideways and then, finally, downwards to expel any trapped air.

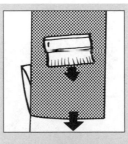

❸ Unfold the lower half and brush down the wall, checking that the edge of the paper aligns with the vertical line marked on the wall.

❹ If any large bubbles remain, peel back the paper while it is still wet and smooth it down again as in step 2.

TRADE TIPS

Allowing the paste to soak into the paper before hanging helps to prevent bubbles.

Trimming the paper ...

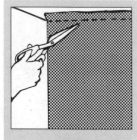

❶

Using the tip of closed scissors, score the paper at the ceiling edge to create a guide for cutting.

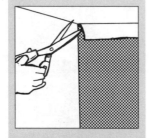

❷

Gently peel back the paper from the ceiling edge and cut along the scored line. Smooth the paper back into place.

❸

Score and trim in the same way at the bottom edge. Wipe any paste off the skirting board.

❹

Hang the next length in the same way, lining it up to the first length and matching any patterns. The edges must meet, but not overlap.

TRADE TIPS

Use your finger wrapped in a handkerchief to flatten wallpaper seams.

Papering around sockets and switches

❶

Paste and hang the length of paper, smoothing the top end down to the top of the switch. Press the paper against the switch to check its position.

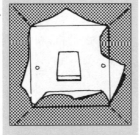

❷

Using small scissors, make four diagonal cuts from the centre of the switch fitting to about 1 cm/ ½ in beyond the corners.

❸

Mark around the switch plate with the back of a pair of scissors. Cut off the excess and brush the paper back into place.

If you prefer to paper behind the switch, turn off the electricity at the mains fuse box, loosen the screws in the switch plate and paste and cut as above, tucking waste behind the plate, then tighten the screws.

TRADE TIPS

When decorating, wear an apron with big pockets – very handy for carrying tools, etc.

Papering round corners

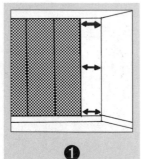

❶

Always paper corners in two parts. Measure from the last length to the corner at the top, middle and bottom. Add 1 cm / ½ in to the widest measurement to allow for overlap around the corner.

❷

Cut the next prepared length to this measurement and set aside the offcut for the next wall.

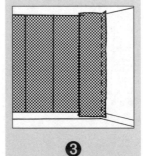

❸

Paste and hang the measured piece, brushing the 1 cm / ½ in overlap around the corner on to the adjacent wall. Trim top and bottom.

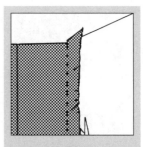

❹

If necessary, snip the edges of the overlap to encourage it to lie flat.

If you do not have a trough, soak ready-pasted paper in the bath.

Papering round corners (continued)

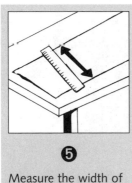

❺ Measure the width of the offcut.

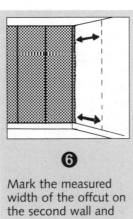

❻ Mark the measured width of the offcut on the second wall and draw a line vertical to this width for guidance.

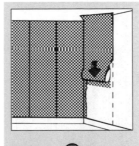

❼ Paste and hang the offcut, ensuring that the uncut edge follows the vertical line. Brush into the corner, covering the overlap. Trim top and bottom.

TRADE TIPS

A glue stick is very handy for gluing edges.

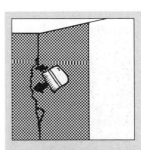

❽ If the paper is out of true, brush the offcut into the corner, allowing it to extend on to the completed wall. Then crease the corner with the back of a pair of scissors, peel back the paper and cut off the waste.

Papering into window recesses

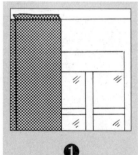

❶

Paste and hang a full length of paper, allowing the drop to hang over the window.

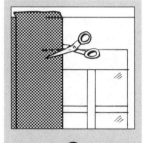

❷

Cut a horizontal line along the edge of the wall at the top of the window recess. Make a similar cut lower down, along the level of the window sill. Trim the paper round the end of the sill and smooth into place.

❸

Smooth the paper into the recess of the wall. Mark and trim any overlaps as before.

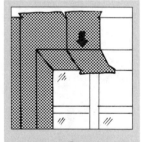

❹

Paste and hang short lengths on the upper part of the wall, marking and trimming the overlaps as before. Trim along the top.

Never rely on a window or door frame as a vertical guide as they are rarely true.

Papering into window recesses (continued)

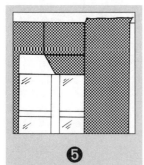

⑤

Paste and hang a full length of paper at the end of the window recess in the same way as on the other side.

⑥

Cut small patches, just slightly oversized, to fill in any gaps left. Don't forget to allow enough for matching patterns.

⑦

Paste and hang the patches, aligning the straight edge with the previously hung short length. Smooth with a paper hanging brush.

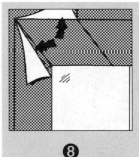

⑧

Tuck in any overlap under the previously hung full length.

When purchasing wallpaper, make sure all rolls have the same batch number.

Papering round doors

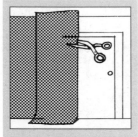

❶

Paste and hang a full length of paper, allowing the drop to hang over the door frame. Cut horizontally to the inner edge of the door frame, allowing an extra 5 cm/2 in to overlap the top of the frame.

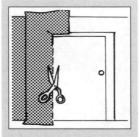

❷

Cut vertically, again allowing 5 cm/2 in overlap. Make a diagonal cut into the top corner of the door frame.

❸

Smooth the paper into the angle of the door frame, stabbing it with the bristles of the brush.

❹

Score and trim the overlaps around the door frame, then those at the ceiling and skirting board. Now, working from the other side of the door, draw a vertical line so that the next length hangs straight.

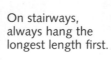

On stairways, always hang the longest length first.

Papering round fireplaces

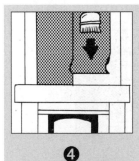

❶ Measure and mark the centre of the chimney breast.

❷ Draw a vertical line through it, using your plumb line (see page 71).

❸ Paste and hang the first length to align with this vertical. Brush the paper down towards the mantelpiece. Score and trim overlaps in the usual way (see page 74).

❹ Paste and hang the second length on the other side of the vertical line.

TRADE TIPS

Allow wallpaper at least 24 hours to dry before replacing wall fittings.

Papering into arches

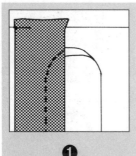

1

Paste and hang the first length to align with the centre of the arch. Cut out the arch shape, allowing a 2.5 cm/1 in overlap to turn into the arch.

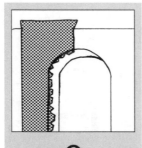

2

Make small cuts along the overlap, then turn it in to lay flat on the inside of the arch. Score and trim overlaps at the ceiling edge. Hang the second length in the same way.

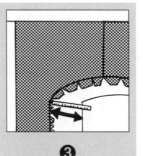

3

Measure the depth of the arch at the bottom and top. Using the larger measurement (the walls may not be true), cut two lengths of paper to meet at the top.

4

Paste and hang the paper on the inside of the arch, brushing upwards to make a neat join at the top. Score and trim any excess at the sides and bottom.

TRADE TIPS

Leftover wallpaper can be used to line drawers.

Papering behind radiators

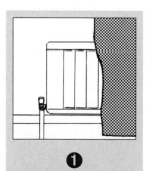

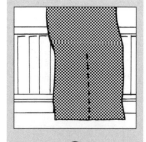

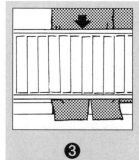

❶ Paste and hang a full length of paper, allowing the lower half to drape loosely over the radiator.

❷ Cut the paper to align with the brackets at the back of the radiator.

❸ Lower the paper behind the radiator, allowing the cut to fall on either side of the bracket.

❹ Smooth the paper using a radiator roller. Score and trim the overlaps in the usual way.

Make a radiator roller with a broom handle wrapped in a clean rag.

Wallpaper notes

5
PAINTING

Preparation

To get the best results when painting, you will have to spend time on the preparations: this means preparing the area, to protect it from the mess you are about to make, and also preparing the surface to be painted. It is well worth spending time filling and rubbing down an uneven surface to get a really smooth finish.

Clear the room and prepare the surfaces

❶

Prepare the room by removing curtains, pictures, etc. Stack furniture in the centre of the room and cover it with dustsheets.

❷

Fill in any cracks in walls or woodwork, using the appropriate filler. Allow these areas to dry and rub them lightly with sandpaper for a smooth finish. Scrape off any loose, flaking paint and sand surfaces to a smooth finish.

❸

Lightly sand down any areas of painted wood to roughen the surface, which creates a better bond for new paint.

❹

Wash all the walls and woodwork with warm water and detergent. Rinse and dry thoroughly.

To smooth filler into edges and corners, use a wet finger.

Make sure you choose the right paint for the job: for ceilings and walls, use several coats of emulsion; for woodwork, use undercoat, then gloss (new wood will need a coat of primer first).

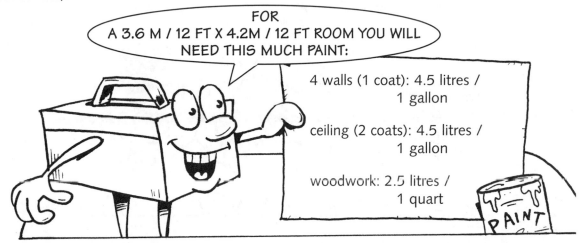

FOR A 3.6 M / 12 FT X 4.2M / 12 FT ROOM YOU WILL NEED THIS MUCH PAINT:

4 walls (1 coat): 4.5 litres / 1 gallon

ceiling (2 coats): 4.5 litres / 1 gallon

woodwork: 2.5 litres / 1 quart

Clear the room

Prepare the paint

❶

Vacuum up all dust and debris.

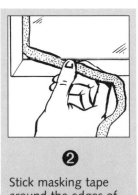

❷

Stick masking tape around the edges of the floor covering and around the window panes to protect them from smudges.

To prepare the paint, stir it thoroughly with a clean stick (except non-drip paint).

TRADE TIPS

To get rid of skin or debris on an open tin of paint, strain it, using an old pair of tights stretched over a paint kettle or tin.

Ceilings

Painting ceilings with a brush

①

Divide the ceiling into sections that run parallel to the window and paint these in sequence.

②

Load the correct size of brush (see page 104) with paint, covering only a third of the bristle area. Drain off any excess paint.

③

Using a 50 mm/2 in brush, paint in a narrow strip along the ceiling edge parallel to the window, and continue a short way along the other wall. This is known as 'cutting in.'

④

Using a 125 mm/5 in brush, brush away from the edge with sweeping strokes to fill in the first section. Continue to work across the ceiling, section by section. Brush-marks do not show when emulsion paint has dried.

TRADE TIPS

Wear a shower cap when painting ceilings to keep paint off your hair.

Painting ceilings with a roller

Non-drip emulsion

❶

Pour the emulsion into the deep end of the paint tray. Dip the roller in, then drain off excess paint by rolling it up and down the sloping ramp.

❷

Using a 50 mm/2 in brush, paint along the ceiling edge parallel to the window, and continue a short way along the ceiling above the other wall.

❸

Fill in the rest of the section with a roller, using criss-cross strokes to spread the paint.

Solid emulsion is non-drip, comes in its own tray, and needs no stirring. It is very convenient to use, but a little expensive.

Prepare a new roller by soaking in soapy water for a few hours to release odd bits of fibre. Rinse and dry before use.

Painting Walls

YOU CAN CHOOSE SILK OR MATT EMULSION

Painting walls with a brush

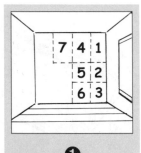

❶ Mentally divide the wall into numbered sections that guide the painting sequence. You will start at the top of the wall nearest the window.

❷ Using a 50 mm/2 in brush, cut in along the wall and ceiling edge. Windows and door frames should be edged completely before you paint the surrounding walls.

❸ Load a 100 mm/4 in brush, and apply the paint in two strips, the upper one in one direction, the lower one in the other direction.

❹ Without loading the brush with more paint, lightly brush downwards to finish off the section. Repeat this procedure for each of the remaining sections.

TRADE TIPS

For short breaks when using emulsion, wrap the brush or roller in kitchen foil to prevent the paint from drying hard.

Painting walls with a roller

Behind radiators

❶

Start at the top corner nearest the window. You are going to work downwards, section by section.

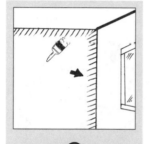

❷

Using a 50 mm/2 in brush, cut in along the ceiling and wall edge.

❸

Fill in the rest of the section, using criss-cross strokes with a roller to spread the paint and finishing off with straight strokes in one direction.

You can buy a special slim roller from DIY stores to paint behind radiators.

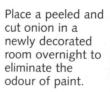

Place a peeled and cut onion in a newly decorated room overnight to eliminate the odour of paint.

Window Frames

Painting sequence

Casement windows

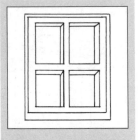

Start with the rebates and finish with the window sill.

Sash windows

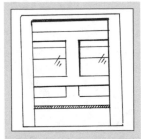

Sash windows are best painted in two stages (see opposite page).

Masking

If you use masking tape, leave a 3 mm / $\frac{1}{8}$ in gap to allow a little paint to settle on the glass. This will seal the join with the frame to eliminate any damp.

A plastic shield is very useful to protect the glass from paint. Always wipe paint off the shield each time you move it.

TRADE TIPS

Work a new brush to and fro across your hand to dislodge loose hairs before you dip it in the paint.

Painting the frames

1

Load a 25 mm/1 in brush, angled if you have one, with prepared paint.

2

Cut in, allowing the paint to overlap about 3 mm/ ⅛ in on to the glass to seal out any damp.

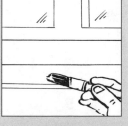

3

Complete painting the window, in the correct order, using the appropriate size of brush and finishing with the window sill.

Sash windows

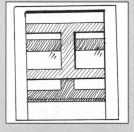

To paint sash windows, partially open both windows and paint all the exposed parts. Allow these areas to dry, then reverse the position of the windows and complete the painting.

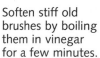

Soften stiff old brushes by boiling them in vinegar for a few minutes.

Doors

FLUSH DOORS NEED TO BE PAINTED IN SECTIONS SO IMAGINE THEM DIVIDED UP LIKE THIS

Painting flush doors

❶

Remove any door furniture and place newspaper under the door to protect the floor from drips. Wedge the door open – use a screwdriver if you don't have any plastic wedges.

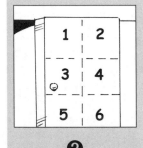

❷

Start at the top of the door and work downwards, painting section by section, as above.

❸

Load a 75 mm/3 in brush with prepared paint, covering only a third of the bristles. Drain off any excess paint.

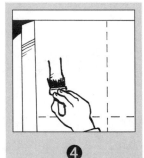

❹

Paint the first square, brushing up and down, then across and back.

To prevent a skin forming, seal tins of paint tightly and store upside-down.

Painting flush doors (continued)

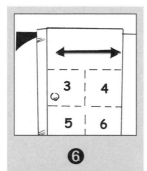

5

Paint the second square, brushing up and down, then across and back.

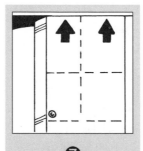

6

Without reloading the brush, brush back and forth across the width of the door.

7

Again, without reloading the brush, brush these two squares with a very light upwards movement.

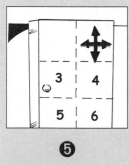

8

Complete the rest of the door in the same way, painting the edge of the door and the frame last. To clean brushes, see page 104.

TRADE TIPS

Check doors for runs as soon as you have finished painting. Brush them out while they are still wet, with light upward strokes.

Painting panelled doors

❶

Remove any door furniture and place newspaper under the door to protect the floor from drips. Wedge the door open.

❷

Start with the panels and finish with the frame.

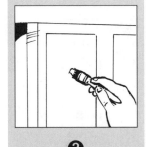

❸

Load a 75 mm/3 in brush with prepared paint, covering only a third of the bristles. Drain off any excess paint.

❹

Paint the panels in sections as you would a flush door (see pages 98–9).

TRADE TIPS

For short breaks when using oil-based paint, wrap brushes in a cloth dampened with white spirit.

Painting panelled doors (continued)

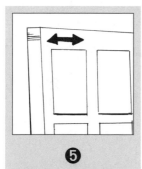

❺

Paint the bars in three stages, a small strip at a time, without reloading your brush. First, brush back and forth until the brush becomes dry.

❻

Next, brush up and down.

❼

Finally, brush across in one direction, using very light strokes to give a smooth finish. Reload the brush, then begin the next strip.

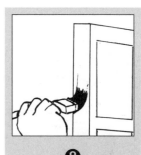

❽

Using a 25 mm/1 in brush, paint the edges and, finally, the frame.

To leave brushes overnight when using oil-based paint, wipe off as much paint as possible, place the brush in a sealed plastic bag and lie it flat.

Finishing with gloss paint

❶

Lightly sand the thoroughly dry undercoat using fine sandpaper, then wipe clean with a dry cloth.

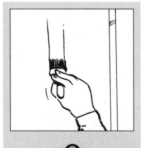

❷

Apply the gloss paint evenly and quite thickly; however, don't put too much paint on the brush as this may cause runs.

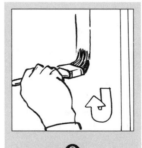

❸

Finish off the gloss paint with long, light vertical strokes, ending with an upward stroke.

❹

If your work is full, of runs, sags, wrinkles, etc, leave the paint to harden for a week, then rub down lightly with fine sandpaper, dust with a dry cloth and apply fresh gloss paint.

TRADE TIPS

To check whether gloss paint is dry, run your fingernail across it.

Textured paint

Textured paint is easy to apply and will hide small bumps, cracks and imperfections; it is very useful where you have a large area of poor quality to cover. But beware, it is extremely difficult to remove.

COVER-UP JOBS ARE MY SPECIALITY

Applying textured paint

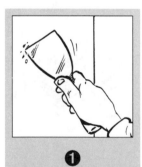

❶

Scrape off any loose paint.

❷

Use a roller to apply the textured paint, as this will coat the wall more thickly than a brush.

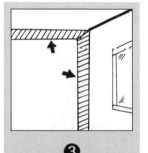

❸

Use a 50 mm/2 in brush to cut in (see page 92), following the same procedure as for ordinary emulsion paints.

❹

Plastic scrapers and combs are available from DIY stores to create different effects.

Use a matt finish to disguise bumps and hollows – a shiny emulsion will highlight faults.

Brushes

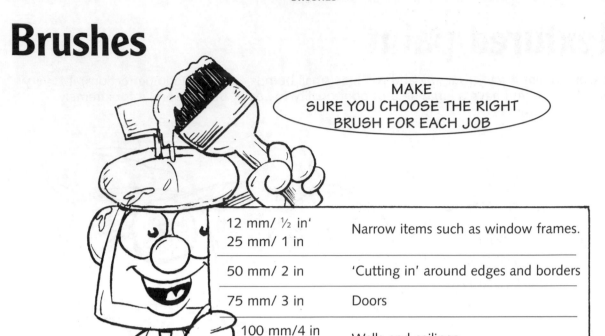

MAKE SURE YOU CHOOSE THE RIGHT BRUSH FOR EACH JOB

12 mm/ ½ in' 25 mm/ 1 in	Narrow items such as window frames.
50 mm/ 2 in	'Cutting in' around edges and borders
75 mm/ 3 in	Doors
100 mm/4 in 125 mm/5 in	Walls and ceilings.

Cleaning brushes

❶

Remove any excess paint from the brushes by working them to and fro on newspaper.

❷

Rinse the brushes, using water to remove water-based paint and white spirit for oil-based paint. (Check the label on the tin if you are in doubt.)

❸

Now wash the brushes in warm, soapy water.

❹

Finally, rinse them thoroughly under cold running water, then dry with a clean cloth.

TRADE TIPS

When storing brushes, wrap them in kitchen paper and lay them flat.

Rollers

Rollers are used almost exclusively for applying emulsion paint over large areas. Keep them clean, or they will become dry and will not absorb or apply paint evenly.

ALL EMULSION PAINT IS WATER BASED

Cleaning rollers

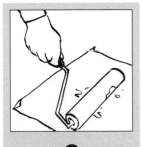

❶ Remove any excess paint by rolling over kitchen paper. Remove the roller sleeve from the handle.

❷ For water-based paint, rinse the sleeve under cold running water.

For oil-based paint, soak the sleeve in white spirit.

❸ Wash the sleeve in warm, soapy water. Rinse, and dry it with a clean cloth.

TRADE TIPS

Non-drip gloss can be removed from a roller or brush with soapy water if you act quickly.

Painting notes

6

ODD JOBS

Replacing window panes

MEASURE CAREFULLY SO YOU BUY THE RIGHT SIZE PANE

When you need to replace a window pane, measure the height and width of the area to be glazed, then ask the glazier to cut the right size.

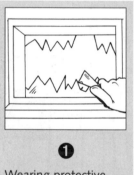

❶

Wearing protective gloves, remove all broken glass.

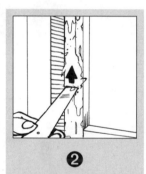

❷

Using a chisel, remove the old putty from the rebate.

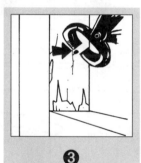

❸

Pull out the panel pins with pincers or pliers and save the pins for re-use.

❹

Brush the rebate clean, then paint it with a suitable primer and allow it to dry.

If transporting glass in a car, wrap each pane separately in a blanket or newspaper to help prevent breakage.

Replacing window panes (continued)

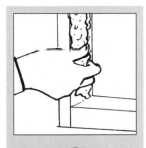

5

Press the new putty around the frame rebate working it in with your thumbs. Make it about 3 mm/⅛ in thick.

6

Position the new pane in the rebate and press gently around the edges to set it into the putty.

7

Tap in the panel pins at about 23 cm/9 in intervals.

8

Press more putty around the edge of the glass, again using your thumb.

Should glass break while you are working, never try to catch it – just let it fall.

Replacing window panes (continued)

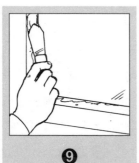

9

Using the straight edge of a putty knife, smooth the putty.

10

With the edge of the putty knife, trim any excess putty off the glass and mitre each corner.

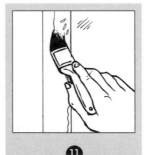

11

Dip a brush in water and lightly run it along the putty to seal it.

12

A week later, when the putty has hardened, paint it, allowing a 3 mm/⅛ in overlap on to the glass to seal the joint from damp.

TRADE TIPS

For super-shiny windows, look for a brand of cleaning fluid to which vinegar has been added to give shine and prevent smears.

Replacing leaded lights

MEASURE THE DIMENSIONS OF THE PANES *AFTER* THE LEAD STRIPS HAVE BEEN OPENED

❶ Prise open the lead strips with a sharp knife or a chisel and remove the broken pane of glass. Remove the old putty from the rebate using a chisel.

❷ Work new, soft, pliable putty into the surround, using your thumb.

❸ Slot the new pane into the bed of fresh putty.

❹ Using a putty knife, carefully press the lead strips back over the pane of glass, and trim off the excess putty.

TRADE TIPS

When it has dried, blacken the putty on leaded lights with black shoe polish.

Filling damaged window sills

❶

Using a chisel, scrape out all wood that is rotten and soft.

❷

Brush out this loose wood and dust the sill. Allow the remaining sound wood to dry thoroughly.

❸

Using a filler knife, smooth an appropriate filler into the indent and allow it to dry.

❹

Sand the sill until the finish is very smooth, ready for painting.

Always sand along the grain of the wood, not across it.

Fixing a wall cabinet

THIS PIECE OF TAPE SHOWS WHEN I REACH THE RIGHT DEPTH IN THE WALL

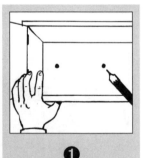

❶

To mark fixing points, hold the cabinet against the wall and poke a pencil through the fixing holes in the back, to mark the wall.

❷

Using a hand or electric drill, make holes deep enough to take a wall plug and screw. Always make sure wall plugs are the correct size for the screws.

❸

Tap in the wall plugs with a hammer until they are flush with the wall surface.

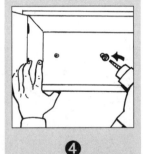

❹

Position the cabinet on the wall, then drive the screws through the holes in the back of it, into the plugged wall.

Spent matches can be used as a substitute for wall plugs when screwing lightweight fixings into wood, e.g. on a door handle.

Putting up a shelf

When fixing a shelf, use brackets that reach as far as possible across the width of the shelf and fix them about 75 cms / 30 in apart. If the shelf has to carry a lot of weight, fit them closer together.

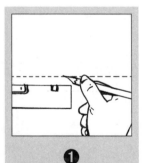

❶

Use a spirit level to draw a horizontal line the exact height and the length required for the shelf.

❷

Measure the distance from the end of the shelf to the bracket position. Place the bracket directly beneath the horizontal line and poke a pencil through the holes to mark the wall. Repeat for the other bracket.

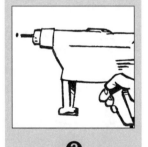

❸

Using an electric or hand drill, make holes deep enough to take a wall plug and screw (approximately 4 cm/ 1½ in).

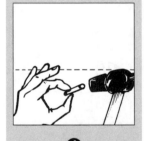

❹

Tap in the wall plugs with a hammer until they are flush with the wall surface.

TRADE TIPS

When using adhesive hooks, always ensure that the surface is clean and dry before sticking hooks on.

REMEMBER,
THE HEAVIER THE LOAD,
THE MORE BRACKETS YOU'LL
NEED

Putting up a shelf (continued)

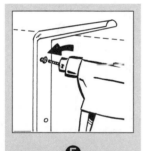

❺

Drive the screws through the brackets into the plugged wall and tighten to secure them to the wall.

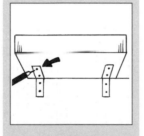

❻

Rest the shelf on the brackets and poke a pencil through the holes of the bracket to mark the fixing holes on the shelf.

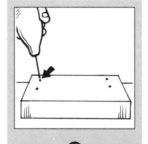

❼

Remove the shelf and use a bradawl (a pointed woodworking tool) to make small starter holes in the shelf to help you to fix the screws.

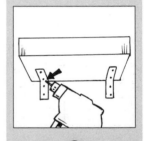

❽

Drive the screws through the brackets into the shelf.

TRADE TIPS

Remember when turning a screwdriver, 'Right is tight, left is loose.'

Fixing a curtain rail

LET THE SUN SHINE IN!

When measuring for a curtain rail, allow an extra 22.– 30 cm / 9 – 12 in at each side of the window so that curtains can be drawn right back.

❶

Mark the required height of the rail, which is normally about 5 cm/2 in above the window. Continue the marks at intervals across the window.

❷

Join up the marks with a line that extends 23–31 cm/9–12 in beyond each side of the window frame.

❸

Mark the position of the brackets, starting 5 cm/ 2 in from each end and spacing the others about 30 cm/12 in apart.

❹

Using an electric or hand drill, drill holes at each bracket position, deep enough to take a wall plug and screw.

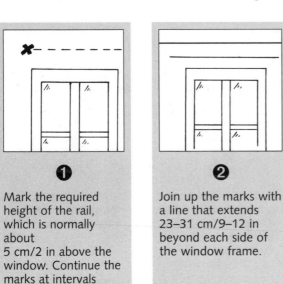

TRADE TIPS

Use furniture polish on your curtain tracks to make curtains run easily.

Fixing a curtain rail (continued)

Brackets for poles should be fixed 10 cm / 4 in from each end. Long poles will need one in the centre too.

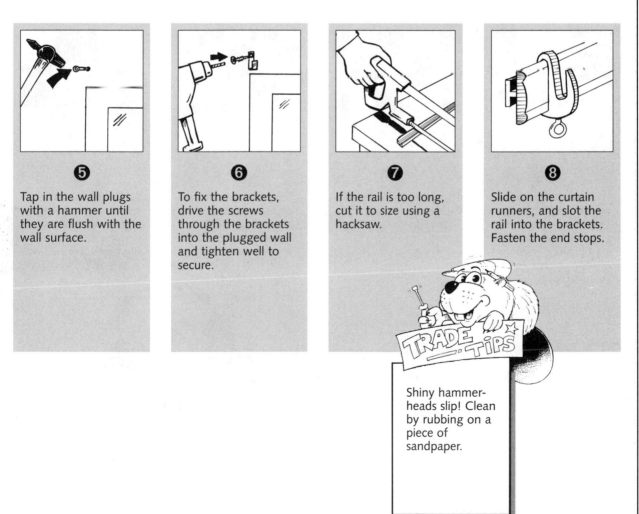

❺ Tap in the wall plugs with a hammer until they are flush with the wall surface.

❻ To fix the brackets, drive the screws through the brackets into the plugged wall and tighten well to secure.

❼ If the rail is too long, cut it to size using a hacksaw.

❽ Slide on the curtain runners, and slot the rail into the brackets. Fasten the end stops.

TRADE TIPS

Shiny hammer-heads slip! Clean by rubbing on a piece of sandpaper.

Sealing gaps

Flexible sealant is easy to use and is available in a variety of colours.

Flexible sealant

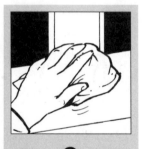

❶

To prepare the surface, remove any old sealant, clean off grease and dirt with washing-up liquid and dry the surface thoroughly.

❷

Squeeze flexible waterproof sealant well into the gap.

❸

Using a moistened finger, smooth the sealant into a neat, concave shape.

❹

Any messy surplus may be wiped away with a clean tissue. If the sealant has hardened, trim it away with a sharp knife or razor blade.

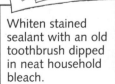

Whiten stained sealant with an old toothbrush dipped in neat household bleach.

Self-adhesive plastic is very easy to use and makes no mess – just press it into place.

EVEN I CAN'T MAKE A MESS WITH THIS

Plastic strip

❶

Prepare the surface as step 1 on page 118. Cut the strip with scissors to the required length.

❷

Peel back the liner a few inches from the end of the strip and position the strip along the edge of the bath or basin.

❸

Press the adhesive strip firmly into the gap to be sealed. Continue, gradually peeling back the strip a little at a time, to the end.

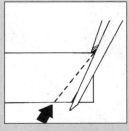

❹

If you come to a corner, cut the end of the strip at an angle of 45°. Reverse the angle on the strip to be joined on. Remove adhesive and push the angled sections firmly together.

TRADE TIPS

Pour boiling vinegar over stains caused by dripping taps.

Ceramic trim tiles

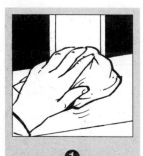

❶

All surfaces must be sound, dry and clean to ensure the tiles adhere firmly.

❷

To affix the first mitred corner tile, apply adhesive to the two flat edges at the back of the tile, i.e. top and bottom.

❸

Firmly position the tile with its mitred end pointing into the corner.

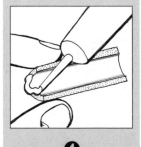

❹

To affix the second mitred corner tile, apply adhesive on the two flat edges and the mitred edge.

TRADE TIPS

You can buy ready-to-fix packs of ceramic trim tiles which include the adhesive sealant in many colours to match your bathroom.

USE WATERPROOF ADHESIVE WHEN TILING BATHROOMS AND KITCHENS

Ceramic trim tiles (continued)

❺ Lay the second mitred tile, butted against the first, to complete the corner. Repeat the process in the other corners.

❻ Now work from the corners towards the centre to fill in the sides of the bath. Apply adhesive to the rounded-end tile and place it next to the corner tile.

❼ Apply adhesive to the remaining tiles and work towards the centre, cutting the last tile to fit the centre gap.

❽ Trim off excess adhesive with a sharp knife. Leave to dry (normally 24 hours). Fill in joints between tiles with water-resistant grout using a sponge (see page 123).

TRADE TIPS

Clean stained grouting on wall tiles with neat household bleach applied on an old toothbrush.

Replacing damaged tiles

When buying replacement tiles, take an old one with you to be sure you get the right colour.

①

Carefully dig out the old grouting around the damaged tile, using an old screwdriver.

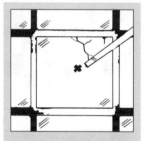

②

To remove the damaged tile, use a hammer and and old screwdriver to chip away at it, starting at the centre.

③

Use the screwdriver to dig out any remaining adhesive from the wall space.

④

Using a plastic tile adhesive comb, apply fresh adhesive to the wall space.

TRADE TIPS

If old tiles are in good condition, you can fix new ones on top or paint them with enamel paint.

Replacing damaged tiles (continued)

When drilling a hole in a tile, stick plastic tape on the surface to stop the drill slipping.

❺

Apply adhesive to the back of the new tile.

❻

Press the tile into position, placing matchsticks between the joints, and leave it overnight to allow the adhesive to set.

❼

With a sponge, smear grouting paste into the joints between the tiles.

❽

Leave the grouting to dry for 24 hours, and then polish the surface with a clean, dry cloth.

When drilling tiles, always use a slow drill speed.

Cutting tiles

❶

Using a straight edge, score a deep line on the glazed side of the tile, with a tile cutter.

❷

Place the tile with the scored line over two matchsticks, then very gently press down.

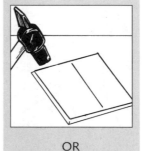

OR

Score a line with a tile cutter, then tap sharply just behind this score line.

OR

Score a line with a tile cutter, then use pincers to snap off a section of tile.

When cutting tiles only score one line. A second attempt could result in an uneven break.

Fixing a smoke alarm

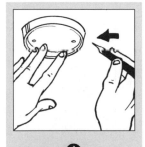

❶ Hold the base against the ceiling and mark the screw hole positions, using a pencil.

❷ Drill through the centre of the marked screw holes.

❸ Push plastic wall plugs firmly into the holes.

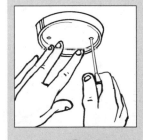

❹ Drive the screws through the base into the plugged ceiling holes. Assemble the alarm and test it.

Test all alarms once a week, and on returning from holiday.

Draught-proofing

Door and window frames

Adhesive draught-proofing strip will stick to any clean, dry surface.

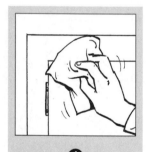

❶

Clean and thoroughly dry the area to be sealed.

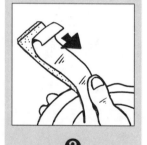

❷

Unwind about 40 cm/15 in from the plastic foam strip. Peel back the backing paper.

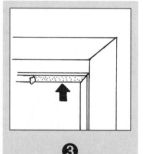

❸

Press the sticky side of the foam strip to the top of the door frame surface. Continue to peel and press on the strip, working down to the bottom of the door.

❹

Using scissors, cut the foam strip neatly to the required length.

To keep draughts at bay, renew plastic foam draught excluder every two years.

Doors

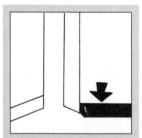

FELT RIBBON PLASTIC STRIP
(self-adhesive)

Cut to length, then press on to the bottom of the door, allowing the felt to fit snugly against the floor.

BRUSH DRAUGHT EXCLUDER

Cut to length, position and screw into place so that the brush sweeps the floor.

Letter boxes

DOUBLE BRUSH DRAUGHT EXCLUDER

Place over the letter box opening on the inside of the door and screw into place.

Fireplaces

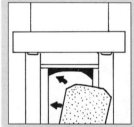

BOARD DRAUGHT EXCLUDER

Cut and fix cardboard to the exact size of the gap.

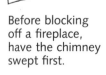

Before blocking off a fireplace, have the chimney swept first.

Stairs

Fixing creaking stairs from underneath (if accessible)

Loose wooden blocks

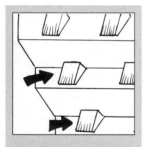

Prise off any blocks that are loose, and reattach them using wood adhesive.

Missing blocks

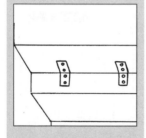

Replace with shelf brackets, which make excellent substitutes.

Loose wedges

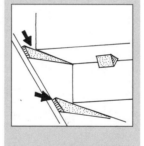

Hammer any that are loose back into position.

Still creaking

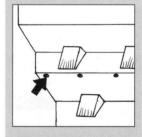

Insert screws upwards through the tread into the riser.

Rubbing screws with Vaseline or soap makes them easier to screw in or out.

Fixing creaking stairs from above

❶

Roll up and remove any stair covering from the offending stair tread.

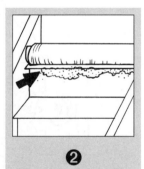

❷

Puff some talcum powder into the joints.

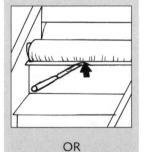

OR

Lift the tread away from the riser with a chisel and insert wood glue. Remove the chisel.

then

Hammer nails at an angle through the glued tread into the riser, making sure the nail heads are punched below the surface.

TRADE TIPS

Stair carpets need dense pile. Test samples by bending backwards to see if backing shows through.

Security

Putting in a spy hole

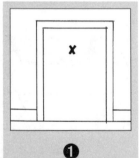

❶

Spy holes are usually placed at eye level in the centre of the door. Mark this spot with a pencil.

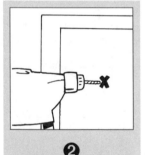

❷

Keeping the drill level, drill a hole through the door at the marked position.

❸

Unscrew the spy hole from the tube extension, and push the spy hole through the drilled hole from the outside.

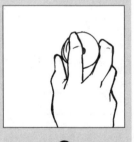

❹

Screw the tube extension tightly to the spy hole on the inside of the door.

TRADE TIPS

When going out, deter burglars by waving and shouting goodbye to an imaginary person left in the house.

Fixing a door chain

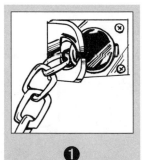

❶

Position the locking plate close to the opening edge of the door, always keeping the plate horizontal. Prepare the first fixing hole using a bradawl, then fix the screw. Repeat for each screw.

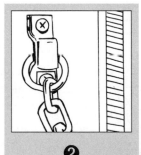

❷

Position the staple and chain on the door frame with the lip at the top near to the edge of the frame. Secure with screws.

Keep hedges trimmed as low as possible, so that anyone trying to break in can be easily seen.

Installing a timeswitch

❶

Switch off the mains electricity at the fuse box (see pages 36–7) and double check that the power is off by trying light switches.

❷

To remove the old switch, undo screws to release the plate.

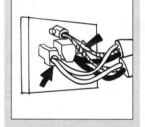

❸

Disconnect the wires from the existing plate without disturbing the yellow and green earth wire connected to the wall box.

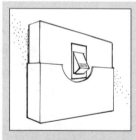

❹

Reconnect the wires to the new security switch, following the manufacturer's instructions. Reassemble the switch and turn on mains electricity.

TRADE TIPS

When leaving the house empty at night, leave living room and bedroom lights on. Leaving a transistor radio on is also a good idea.

Odd job notes

7

CAR MAINTENANCE

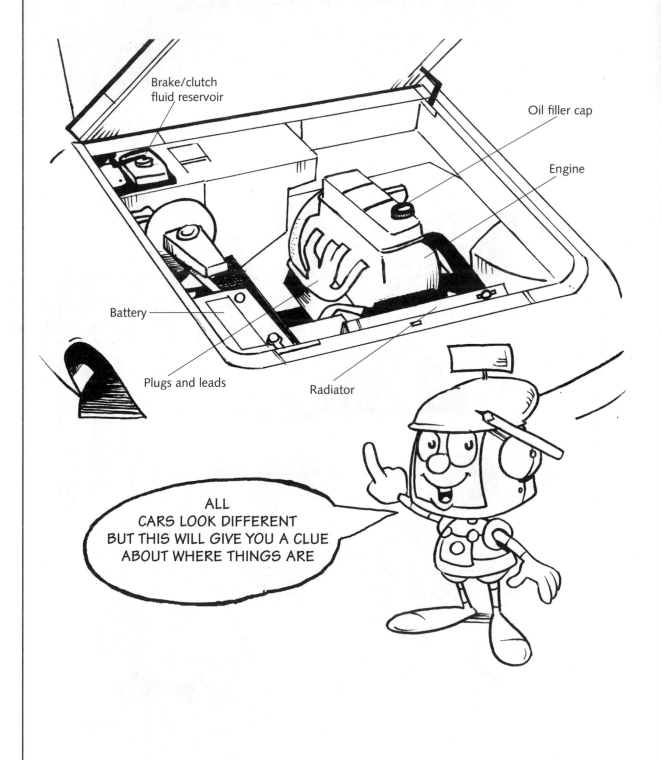

Regular checks

CHECK
THE OIL LEVEL REGULARLY
AND ALWAYS BEFORE LONG
JOURNEYS

Oil level

❶ Park the car on a level surface, switch off the engine, wait a few minutes, then lift up the bonnet.

❷ Pull out the dipstick (check its location in your handbook). Wipe it clean, then reinsert.

❸ Remove the dipstick again and read the oil level. This should always be between the 'min' and 'max' marks.

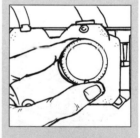

❹ If the oil level is too low, remove the oil cap, located on the top of the engine (see page 136). Top it up with the appropriate oil and replace the cap securely.

TRADE TIPS

From 'min' to 'max' on the dipstick represents about one litre of oil.

Water level

❶

If you have an older car, the filler cap will be situated on the radiator. Remove the cap. The water level should be about 2.5 cm/1 in below the filler hole, so top up as necessary. See engine diagram on page 136.

❷

On most modern cars the radiator cap is situated on an expansion tank or a bottle on which the water level is plainly visible. Top up as necessary.

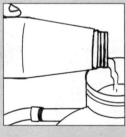

❸

Sometimes called coolant, anti-freeze should be used all year round. If you lose your water you lose your anti-freeze, so add the appropriate amount (one part anti-freeze to two parts water).

TRADE TIPS

Never remove the radiator cap while the engine is hot.

Battery level

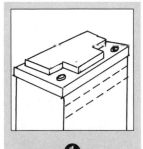

❶

If the battery has level markings, check that the level is between the upper and lower markings.

'Sealed for life' batteries require no attention.

❷

If the battery has no level markings, take off each cell cap or cover and check that the fluid just covers the metal plates visible in each cell.

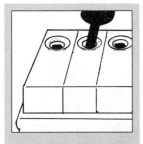

❸

If the level is low, remove the cell caps or cover and top up each cell to the correct level with distilled water.

❹

Check that the small ventilating hole in the cap is not blocked. Replace the caps securely.

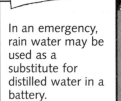

In an emergency, rain water may be used as a substitute for distilled water in a battery.

Washers and wipers

Keep your windscreen and your lights clean – and remember, it's illegal to drive with your washer bottle empty.

1

Locate the washer bottle (see page 136) and check the fluid level in the container. It should be at least half full.

2

If the fluid level is low, refill the bottle with a mixture of screen wash and water. Washing-up liquid is a good substitute for screen wash, but only use a few drops.

3

Clean your wipers whenever you wash the windscreen. Dirty rubbers scratch windows.

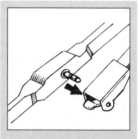

4

Replacement wiper blades are easy to fit and are readily available in different sizes from car accessory shops. Simply unclip the old blade and slide on a new one.

TRADE TIPS

Add a little methylated spirit to screen washer water to act as an anti-freeze and cleaner.

Brake and clutch fluid

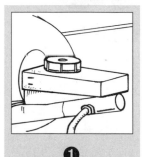

①

The brake and clutch fluid reservoir(s) are normally found inside the engine compartment, on the right-hand side (see page 136).

②

In most modern cars the reservoir(s) are plastic with 'min' and 'max' markings which make it easy to check the level.

③

To check the level on older cars with metal reservoirs, first wipe and then remove the cap. The level should be about 1 cm/½ in below the top of the reservoir.

④

If the level is low, top it up with brake fluid and replace the cap. If there is any sudden significant drop in fluid, contact a garage.

TRADE TIPS

Brake fluid is nasty stuff. Avoid drips or splashes which can irritate skin and eyes and will strip the paint off your car.

Winter driving tips

Floods

Approach flooded roads very slowly. Use a low gear, but keep the revs fairly high to expel water from the exhaust. *It is important not to stall the engine.* When clear of water, apply the brakes hard several times to dry them out. (Check your mirror first!)

Snow

If your car is snowed under, start the engine and clear the snow off the car while it warms up. Start off in second gear, letting the clutch out very gently. If the wheels spin, get out and clear a path. Once the car is in motion, apply gentle pressure to the accelerator. To slow down, use the gears, and brake only when travelling in a straight line.

TRADE TIPS

If your door lock is frozen, use a lighted match to warm the key.

Ice

Drive slowly and gently in the highest possible gear and brake only when travelling in a straight line. If you begin to skid, take your feet off all the pedals and gently steer into the direction of the skid; then accelerate slightly to regain control.

Fog

Drive slowly on the nearside of the road with *dipped* headlights. Keep the windscreen clean and clear, using the washers, wipers and de-misters. Wind down the window for better viewing.

Cover car windows with newspaper at night to prevent them from icing up.

Car maintenance notes

8

CAR TROUBLESHOOTING

It won't start

Flat battery

❶ To check the battery, switch ON the ignition and the headlamps; if they are dim, the battery is faulty.

❷ Switch OFF the ignition and the head-lamps. Remove the covers over the battery terminals and unscrew each terminal. Clean their surfaces using sandpaper, retighten the connections and replace the covers.

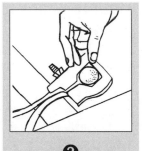

❸ Check that the earth connector is clean and securely attached to the car body or chassis. On modern cars the earth is attached to the negative (–) terminal, but older models may be positively (+) earthed.

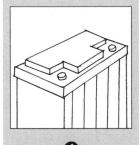

❹ If the car still won't start, or the engine is turning only slowly, it is likely that you have a flat battery. See regular battery checks on page 139.

TRADE TIPS

Keep battery terminals well smeared with Vaseline.

Push starts

❶
You need two people for this, one to drive and one to push! To prepare for the push, press in the clutch, engage second gear, pull out the choke (if there is one) and switch on the ignition.

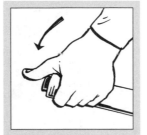

❷
Release the handbrake, ready for the push.

❸
When the car is moving at about 5–10 mph, release the clutch sharply. If the engine does not respond, press in the clutch and repeat the procedure.

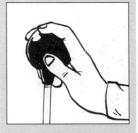

❹
When the engine fires, press in the clutch, brake and take the car out of gear, but keep the engine running by pressing the accelerator.

TRADE TIPS

Stubborn marks on windscreens can be removed using bicarbonate of soda on a damp cloth.

Jump starts

❶ You will need a second car for this. Its battery must be fully charged. Switch OFF both engines.

Put both cars into neutral gear with the handbrakes on.

❷ Connect the red lead to the positive (+) terminals of the two batteries. Attach it to the dead battery first.

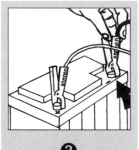

❸ Connect the black lead to the negative (–) terminals.

❹ Start the engine of the healthy car and run it fast for a minute, then leave it idling.

CAUTION – do not let the cars touch.

Jump starts (continued)

❺

Now start the engine of the car with the flat battery and allow it to drop to idling speed.

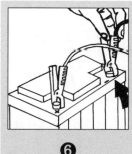

❻

First disconnect the black leads (–) from both batteries.

Then disconnect the red lead (+) from both batteries.

CAUTION – do not allow the jump lead ends to touch.

Damp engine

①

Wipe dry the plug leads, coil and distributor cap and spray them with WD40 or a damp-start aerosol. See engine diagram on page 136.

②

Remove all the plug caps one at a time. Wipe each one clean and dry the inside of the plug cap and the top of the plug (the white covering). If the car still won't start, wait 15 minutes, then try the starter again.

TRADE TIPS

WD40 is also good for squeaky doors and car hinges.

Flooded engine

❶

Press the accelerator pedal *slowly* to the floor and keep it there, but *do not pump*.

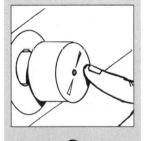

❷

Push in the choke (if applicable).

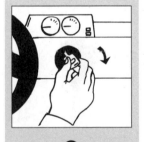

❸

Turn the ignition and allow the engine to spin for about five seconds. Repeat this procedure a few times.

❹

Release the accelerator pedal as soon as the engine fires.

Do not pump the accelerator when starting a car as this causes flooding.

Jammed starter

If your starter is jammed there will be no response from the engine when you turn the ignition key. You will just hear a loud click.

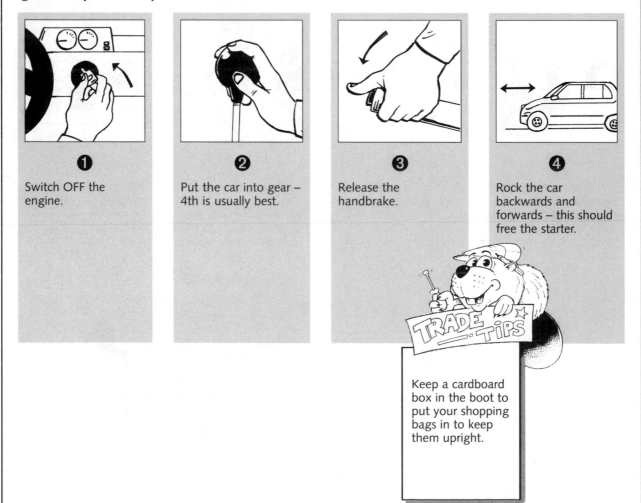

❶ Switch OFF the engine.

❷ Put the car into gear – 4th is usually best.

❸ Release the handbrake.

❹ Rock the car backwards and forwards – this should free the starter.

Keep a cardboard box in the boot to put your shopping bags in to keep them upright.

Heating and cooling

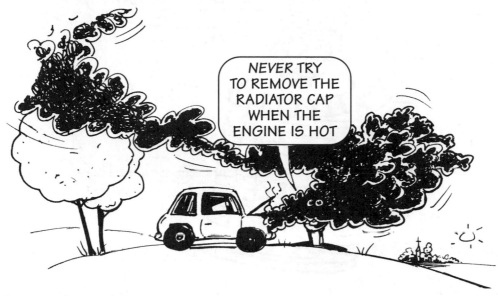

NEVER TRY TO REMOVE THE RADIATOR CAP WHEN THE ENGINE IS HOT

Overheated engine

❶ If your temperature gauge is rising rapidly well above the normal running temperature, pull off the road to a safe place and switch off the engine.

❷ If this is not possible – for example you are stuck in a traffic jam – turn on the heater full blast and pull off the road as soon as possible.

❸ Raise the bonnet very carefully and allow the radiator to cool for 20 to 30 minutes. Do not attempt to remove the radiator cap.

❹ Once the radiator is cool, place a cloth over the radiator cap and gently begin to open it, allowing the steam to escape very slowly. Do this VERY carefully, as boiling water and steam may suddenly spurt out.

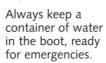

Always keep a container of water in the boot, ready for emergencies.

Overheated engine (continued)

Leaking water

5

After all the steam has escaped, remove the radiator cap.

6

Add enough water to fill the radiator completely. Pour it in gradually or it will gush back out.

7

When you drive on, keep checking the temperature gauge. If it starts rising, stop and check the radiator again.

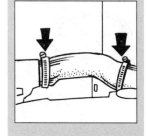

Faulty hoses and radiators are the most common cause of leaks. Check and replace them if they have split. Simply unscrew the jubilee clips which secure the hose, slip it off, slide on a new hose and tighten the clips.

When putting in anti-freeze mix, use two parts water with one part anti-freeze.

Flat tyres

Changing a wheel

❶

Park the car safely on firm, level ground. Switch OFF the engine and switch ON the hazard warning lights.

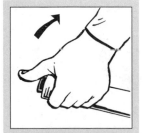

❷

Put the car into first gear or reverse (or P for automatics) and ensure that the handbrake is fully ON.

❸

Locate and remove the spare wheel, jack and tools from the car. Your handbook will tell you where to find them. Place the spare wheel under the car body near the punctured tyre.

❹

Using a screwdriver, lever off the hub cap and trim to reveal the wheel nuts.

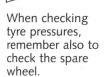

When checking tyre pressures, remember also to check the spare wheel.

YOUR HANDBOOK WILL TELL YOU WHERE TO FIND THE JACK

Changing a wheel (continued)

❺

Using the wheelbrace, slacken but do not remove the wheel nuts in a diagonal order.

❻

Refer to the handbook and place the jack in the 'jack spot' near the punctured tyre.

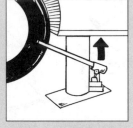

❼

Carefully jack up the car until the tyre is 2.5 cm/ 1 in off the ground.

❽

Remove the wheel nuts, placing them inside the hub cap for safety.

TRADE TIPS

If milk is spilt in the car, apply white vinegar to the stain, allow it to soak in, then wash it out and repeat if the smell persists.

Changing a wheel (continued)

9 Lift the wheel off the studs and roll it to the back of the car.

10 Lift the spare wheel on to the studs. Use your fingers to screw on the wheel nuts with the tapered ends of the nuts facing inwards.

11 Lower the car using the jack. Tighten the nuts securely with the wheelbrace in the order indicated to ensure that the wheel is correctly centred. Replace the hub cap.

12 As soon as possible, check the pressure of the new tyre and have the puncture repaired.

TRADE TIPS

If you have never changed a car wheel, have a practice at home.

Car troubleshooting notes

9
STAINS

BEER

Fresh — Rinse in warm water, then wash as normal.

Dried — Dab with white vinegar, rinse, then soak and wash in biological washing powder.

BLOOD

Fresh — Soak in very salty cold water for 6–12 hours (changing the water frequently), rinse, then wash in cool water.

Dried — Using cool water, soak in biological washing powder overnight and wash as normal.

CANDLE WAX — Scrape off any excess, then place blotting paper or kitchen roll above and below the stain, and iron it with a hot iron to absorb the melted wax. Blot with methylated spirit to remove any remaining colour.

CHEWING GUM — Harden the gum by putting the article in the fridge or freezer, then pick off the cracked gum and treat the stain with methylated or white spirit. Wash as normal.

CHOCOLATE — Scrape off any excess, then soak in cold water and wash in biological washing powder.

Leave newly washed whites hanging out in the sun as long as possible – the sunlight acts as a bleaching agent.

COFFEE

Fresh — Rinse in warm water, then soak and wash in rich, soapy suds.

Dried — Dab the stain with methylated spirit, then soak and wash in rich, soapy suds.

DYE — Saturate with lemon juice, leave for two hours, then wash as normal.

EGG — Mop up the excess with kitchen paper and work a little neat washing-up liquid into the stain. Soak in cold water mixed with biological washing powder and wash on a warm setting.

When soaking a small stain, twist the unstained cloth and put an elastic band around to stop the stain spreading.

FRUIT JUICE

Fresh — Rinse quickly in cold water, then soak and wash in biological washing powder.

Dried — Soften the stain by working a little neat washing-up liquid into it with your finger. Leave for one hour, then soak and wash in biological washing powder.

GRASS — Dab any heavy stains with methylated spirit, then rinse in warm water and wash as normal.

GREASE

Fresh — Press talcum powder on to the greasy mark, leave for a few hours, scrape away any surplus, then brush.

Dried — Scrape off any excess, then use your finger and a little neat washing-up liquid to work at the stain. Soak in warm water and wash with biological washing powder.

ICE CREAM Wipe off any excess, soak in warm biological washing powder and wash as normal.

INK
Felt-tip or ballpoint

Dab repeatedly with methylated spirit, then gently rub in neat washing-up liquid, rinse and wash as normal. If the stain remains, try squeezing lemon juice over it, then cover it with salt. Leave for one hour, rinse and wash.

Fountain pen ink

Soak in milk for 24 hours, then wash as normal. If the stain remains, try squeezing lemon juice over it, then cover it with salt. Leave for one hour, rinse and wash.

LIPSTICK Remove any excess with your fingernail, work in neat washing-up liquid to loosen the stain, and wash as normal.

MASCARA Sponge with neat washing-up liquid, rinse and wash as normal.

MILDEW Soak and wash in biological detergent containing oxygen bleach.

Hot water sets most stains, so always treat them before they go in the washing machine.

MILK

Fresh Rinse well in cold water, then wash on warm with biological washing powder.

Dried Soak well in Biotex detergent before washing.

NAIL VARNISH Blot up any excess, dab with non-oily nail varnish remover, then apply methylated spirit to remove any traces of colour.

OIL Scrape off any excess and work neat washing-up liquid into the stain with your finger. Soak, then wash in warm water with biological washing powder.

Never use spirits or solvents on man-made fibres or rain-proofed fabrics.

PAINT (EMULSION)

Fresh Soak in cold water.

Dried Dab with methylated spirit and wash as normal.

PAINT (GLOSS)

Fresh Dab with white spirit, rinse, then wash.

Dried Moisten with neat washing-up liquid, then sponge with white vinegar. Rinse, then wash.

PENCIL Work neat washing-up liquid into the mark with your finger. Rinse, then wash as normal.

PERFUME

Fresh Rinse in warm water and wash as normal.

Dried Soften with neat washing-up liquid, working it in with your finger. Rinse, then wash as normal.

PERSPIRATION Sponge the stain with white vinegar, rinse, then soak in a biological washing powder solution before washing, or dissolve a couple of aspirins in the washing water.

RUST Dip half a lemon in salt. Rub this over the stain and leave the fabric for about an hour, then rinse and wash as normal.

SCORCH MARKS Soak immediately in cold milk, although bad marks cannot be remedied.

SHOE POLISH Scrape off any excess polish. Dab with white spirit or methylated spirit, rinse and wash as normal.

SPIRITS Rinse in cold water, although stubborn stains may need to be sponged with methylated spirit. Wash as normal.

STICKY LABELS Remove any remains by rubbing with white spirit.

When using a solvent stain remover, always work from the outside of the stain into the centre. Don't rub, just dab.

STICKING PLASTERS	Remove the traces with lemon juice.
TAR	Soften the stain with neat washing-up liquid, working it in with your finger. Leave for one hour, rinse, then wash in soapy water.
TEA	Rinse in warm water or soak in Biotex detergent before washing.

WINE (WHITE)	
Fresh	Rinse in warm water, then wash.
Dried	Moisten by working in neat washing-up liquid with your finger. Soak and wash in biological washing powder.
WINE (RED)	Use kitchen paper to soak up the wine, then shake a large quantity of salt over the stain. Rinse with cold water, then sponge with diluted washing-up liquid. Rinse again, then wash.
URINE	Rinse in cold water, then soak in Biotex detergent before washing.
VOMIT	Rinse under a cold water tap, soak in warm water using biological washing powder and a little disinfectant, then wash as normal.

Try treating unidentifiable stains with glycerine, then wash in cool water with a biological detergent.

Stains notes

10
KITCHEN HINTS

LOOSEN A STUCK CAKE BY STANDING THE TIN OVER A PAN OF BOILING WATER FOR A FEW MINUTES

APPLES
Never buy small fruit as there is too much waste from peel and cores.

AVOCADOS
Prevent avocado dip from discolouring: put the stone back into the mixture and cover with clingfilm. Remove the stone before serving.

BANANAS
Prevent peeled bananas from discolouring by sprinkling them with a little lemon juice.

Don't keep other fruit in the same bowl as bananas – they will go off more quickly.

BEEF
Don't choose pieces with gristle between the fat and lean parts as this indicates an old animal.

Always choose beef with meat of a deep red colour and fat of a light yellow colour.

BISCUITS
Soft biscuits can be made crisp again by popping them into a hot oven for a few minutes. Cool them on a wire tray.

BLACK CURRANTS
Strip blackcurrants or redcurrants from their stems with a fork.

BREAD
Keep bread fresh by putting a washed, dried potato in the bread bin.

Refresh a stale loaf by wrapping it in foil and baking it in a hot oven for about 10 minutes.

CABBAGE
Pop a piece of bread into cabbage cooking water to prevent unpleasant smells.

CAKES
Rather than freeze a large cake whole, cut it into sections and defrost only as much as you require.

Put an iced cake on the upturned lid of the tin and place the container over it. It will be easy to remove!

CASSEROLES
Place a layer of foil between the dish and the lid to prevent liquids boiling over and the lid from getting burned.

CAULIFLOWER
A little milk added to the water while cooking keeps cauliflower white.

DIP EGGS THAT ARE STUCK IN THE BOX INTO COLD WATER AND THE EGGS SHOULD COME FREE

CELERY

Celery leaves make a good flavouring for soups, etc. Dry them in a slow oven, then rub them through a sieve.

Stand celery stalks in iced water for 30 minutes to make them extra crisp.

CHEESE

Always wrap cheese in foil or greaseproof paper to keep it fresh. If cheese has gone hard, grate it. Grated cheese also freezes well.

COFFEE

If you run out of coffee filters, kitchen paper makes a good substitute.

CREAM

Add 5 ml/1 tsp of lemon juice to a small carton of double cream to turn it into sour cream.

CUCUMBER

If cucumber gives you indigestion, try slicing it and sprinkling it with salt. Then leave it for about an hour and rinse off the salt.

CURRY

If a curry is too hot, add a little yoghurt or cream.

EGGS

Whisked egg whites in a mixing bowl will remain stiff for 30 minutes if the bowl is turned upside down on a plate.

Boiled eggs are more easily sliced if the knife is repeatedly dipped in boiling water.

If you are one egg short when making a cake, add 15 ml/1 tsp of vinegar. (This will only work if the recipe contains self-raising flour.)

To make one egg equal three, beat the white and the yolk of the egg separately, then add 5 ml/1 tsp of golden syrup to the yolk.

Leftover yolks can be kept in the fridge for several days if they are covered with cold water.

Leftover whites can be stored for up to two weeks in an airtight container in the fridge.

EGGS

Plastic egg boxes can substitute for ice makers.

You can plant seeds in cardboard egg boxes and put them straight into the soil, still in the cups.

To test for freshness, place eggs in a basin of cold water. If the egg lies on the bottom, it's fresh; if it floats, it's not fresh.

Always store eggs pointed end down in the fridge.

FAT

Use a sheet of kitchen paper to skim the fat off a hot dish.

FISH

When skinning fish, dampen your fingers and dip them in salt. You will now have a good grip.

Thaw frozen fish in milk to give it a freshly caught flavour.

When buying fresh fish, look for bright colour in the eyes and gills and for firmness. It should not have an unpleasant smell.

FLIES

Hang fresh lavender at windows to keep flies at bay.

FLOUR

To turn plain flour into self-raising flour, add 12 ml /2½ tsp of baking powder to 225 g/8 oz of plain flour.

FRUIT (DRIED)

When chopping dried fruit, wet the knife to stop the fruit sticking to the blade.

Soak dried fruit in tea instead of water to enhance the flavour.

Toss dried fruit in flour before adding it to a cake mixture – it will be less likely to sink.

FRIDGE

Wipe the fridge with vinegar to get rid of mildew or unpleasant smells.

GARLIC

To crush garlic without a press, sprinkle salt over chopped cloves of garlic and use the blade of a knife to crush them.

GOOSEBERRIES Use scissors to top and tail gooseberries.

HERBS 5 ml/1 tsp of dried herbs equals 10 ml/2 tsp of fresh herbs.

To dry your own herbs, tie them in bunches, cover with paper bags and hang upside down. When completely dry, rub to remove the stalks and store in jars in a cool, dark place.

Herbs can be frozen. Wash and dry thoroughly, then freeze in small bunches in polythene bags.

JAM If the surface of jam is mouldy, simply remove the mould – the rest of the jam is still edible.

JELLIES To help jellies set more quickly, add a few drops of lemon juice.

LEMONS To freeze sliced lemons ready for your drinks, open-freeze slices on a tray, then transfer them to a plastic freezer bag.

If only a few drops of lemon juice are required, prick a hole with a skewer or knitting needle and squeeze out the required amount. Cover the lemon with clingfilm and put it into the fridge to keep.

To yield twice as much juice, microwave the lemon on High for 30 seconds.

MICROWAVES To eradicate unpleasant smells, heat a bowl of water with a slice of lemon added for about five minutes, then wipe it over with a dry cloth.

MILK Cartons of milk freeze well and can be defrosted in a microwave when needed. Shake well before use.

MILK PANS Rinse your milk pan in cold water before boiling milk to prevent the milk from sticking.

MINCER To remove traces of meat from the mincer, pass a slice of bread through it.

ONIONS Peel onions under running water to help prevent tears.

To rid knives of the smell of onions, wash them in cold water.

To make onions less strong – for use in salads, etc. – soak slices in cold water for 30 minutes before use.

When finely chopped onion is required, grate it – it's quicker.

To peel small onions, put them in boiling water for a minute. The skins will slip off easily.

ORANGES To remove pith more easily, soak oranges in boiling water for five minutes before peeling.

OVEN If food spills in the oven while cooking, sprinkle some salt over it. This makes cleaning easier and helps take the smell away.

To help keep the oven clean, line the shelves and the grill pan with foil. When the foil is dirty, simply discard and renew it.

PARSLEY Fresh parsley will keep for about two weeks in a fridge if tightly wrapped in clingfilm.

Parsley also freezes well.

When using parsley in cooking, try to add about five minutes to the cooking time to avoid a bitter flavour.

PASTA Add a few drops of cooking oil to the boiling water to prevent pasta from sticking together.

A ROUND BOTTLE FILLED WITH COLD WATER MAKES A PERFECT ROLLING PIN

PASTRY Chill pastry in the fridge for half an hour before cooking to prevent it from shrinking during cooking.

PEARS Ripen pears in the airing cupboard.

PIES When making and freezing pies, line dishes with tin foil to allow pies to be lifted out once cooked. Freeze when cold still in the tin foil. The dishes can then be used again.

PEKING DUCK To make the skin of Peking Duck really crispy, use a hair dryer to dry the skin before cooking!

PIPING BAG A plastic bag with the corner cut off makes a good substitute.

POTATOES Jacket potatoes will bake more quickly if a skewer is inserted through them (but don't try this in the microwave).

Jacket potatoes also bake more quickly if put into hot water for 15 minutes before being cooked.

Potatoes cut lengthways cook more quickly than those cut across their width.

If potatoes taste too salty, mash them with beaten egg and lots of milk.

PRUNES Soak and cook prunes in cold tea for extra flavour.

RHUBARB To thaw frozen rhubarb, pour boiling water over it, leave it for 30 minutes, then drain well. This also counteracts acidity.

Sprinkle 15 g/1 tbsp of sugar over 450 g/1 lb of rhubarb and leave it overnight. It can then be cooked without adding water.

OH! I'M RUINED!

RICE — Rice that has gone soggy in cooking can be 'saved' – pack it into a lightly oiled ring mould and bake in a hot oven for 10 minutes. Turn it out on to a plate to serve.

SALT — Put the salt cellar in the fridge to keep it dry and free-running.

SARDINES — Strain sardines and add 5 ml/1 tsp of lemon juice to them to reduce oiliness and add flavour.

SAUCE — Lumpy sauce and gravy can be strained through a sieve.

SAUCEPANS — To clean a stained aluminium saucepan, boil some rhubarb in it.

Tin foil screwed up into a ball makes a good saucepan scourer.

To clean a burnt saucepan, sprinkle thickly with salt and dampen with a little water, leave to soak overnight, then add cold water, bring to the boil and clean as usual.

SAUSAGES — When barbecuing sausages, thread them on to a skewer to make turning simple.

SCONES — Try using yoghurt instead of milk to make lighter scones.

SOUP — If soup is too salty, add a raw, peeled potato during cooking. Remember to remove before serving!

STEW — Don't stir burnt stew which has stuck, but transfer it to a clean saucepan, leaving the burnt deposits behind, and add more liquid.

STOCKCUBES — Keep stockcubes in the fridge – they will crumble more easily.

STEAK — Tenderise tough steak by bashing it with a rolling pin or brushing it with oil and lemon prior to cooking.

SUGAR If brown sugar has gone hard, grate it.

If you run out of caster sugar, grind granulated in a food processor or blender.

Use demerara sugar instead of granulated for a crunchy, flavoursome fruit crumble topping.

SYRUP To weigh syrup, place the tin on the scales and spoon out the syrup until the weight has been reduced by the required amount.

TEA Tea left over in the teapot is good for your houseplants.

TINNED MEAT To make tinned meat easier to slice, keep the tins in the fridge.

TOMATOES Ripen tomatoes by wrapping them in foil for a few days. They may also be ripened in an airing cupboard.

Skin tomatoes by plunging them into boiling water and then into cold. The skins will split, ready to be peeled off.

Overripe tomatoes may be firmed in a bowl of ice-cold water to which a little salt has been added.

Tinned tomatoes are chopped more easily if left in the tin and a sharp knife run through them.

VEGETABLES Overcooked vegetables taste delicious, puréed with butter.

WINE Freeze leftover wine in an ice cube tray for use in cooking.

YORKSHIRE PUDDING To prevent Yorkshire pudding from sticking, sprinkle some pepper on the bottom of the tin.

Kitchen hints notes

11
USEFUL TIPS

AFRICAN VIOLETS Always position in a sunny spot. If not flowering, add extra calcium by using the water from boiled eggs.

ANTS Deter ants by shaking scouring powder at their point of entry to the house.

BARBECUES To keep the grill clean, rub over with a raw potato before use.

BAGS (LEATHER) Use the inside of a banana skin to clean leather bags, then polish up with a cloth.

BEANS Rather than buy seeds, save beans from your own crop. Allow them to dry in their pods, then remove and store them for your next planting.

BLUETAC The easiest way to remove Bluetac from walls is to lift it by pressing with another small ball of Bluetac.

BOTTLES Wear a pair of rubber gloves to get a better grip on a stiff top.

If the cork won't go back into a wine bottle, plunge it into boiling water for a few minutes, then try again.

Cut the tops off soft drinks bottles to make containers for paintbrushes.

BUTTONS Dab the centre of buttons with clear nail varnish to seal the thread.

BULBS When buying bulbs for the garden, always make sure they are nice and firm.

CANDLES Freeze candles about one hour prior to lighting them as they then last much longer and drip less.

CATS Sprinkle talcum powder on cat litter to keep it smelling fresh.

Prevent cats from fouling flower beds by sprinkling lemon peel on the soil.

CHAMOIS Old chamois leathers can be softened in warm water to which a dash of olive oil has been added.

CLINGFILM If you keep clingfilm in the fridge it won't stick to itself.

COATHANGERS Wind elastic bands round the ends of coathangers to stop clothes slipping off.

COMPOST Used tea bags make good compost. Store them in a plastic bag, and when the bag is almost full, seal it and leave it out in the garden to allow the tea bags to rot.

COTTON A squirt of hairspray makes cotton easier to thread.

CROCKERY Keep broken crockery for drainage purposes – in the bottom of flower pots, etc.

CURTAINS Curtains will glide more smoothly if you use furniture polish on the rail.

There is no need to remove curtains when painting window ledges. Just drape them through coat hangers hooked to the rail.

Brighten dull net curtains by putting a denture cleaning tablet into the wash.

CUPS Rub cups with salt to remove tea stains.

DISHCLOTHS Clean a dirty cotton dishcloth quickly by putting it in a large bowl of water with a little washing powder and microwave on High for a few minutes. Alternatively, put it in the dishwasher.

> KEEP
> CUT FLOWERS
> FRESH BY CHANGING
> THE WATER AND SNIPPING A
> LITTLE OFF THE STEMS
> EVERY DAY

DECANTERS
Clean a stained or dull decanter by soaking it overnight with a denture tablet in the water.

DRAWERS
Rub the runners of a sticking drawer with candle wax.

When measuring a drawer for a paper lining, remove the drawer, place it on top of the paper and pencil around the outline of the frame.

DUSTBINS
Sprinkle fresh cat litter into the dustbin to absorb moisture and odours.

DUVETS
Shake feather duvets every day to ensure that the maximum amount of air is trapped inside and that the filling is well distributed.

EGG BOXES
Sow seeds in old egg boxes.

ELASTIC
When replacing worn elastic in a waistband, stitch the end of the new length to the old one and pull it in as you draw the old one out.

FABRIC CONDITIONER SHEETS
Use old fabric conditioner sheets to clean mirrors and windows.

FACE FLANNELS
Freshen face flannels and dishcloths by soaking them in water to which a denture cleaning tablet has been added.

Freshen face flannels by boiling them in water that contains 15 ml/1 tbsp of white vinegar.

FLASKS
Freshen a vacuum flask by filling it with boiling water and one denture cleaning tablet. Leave to soak overnight and rinse well.

To clean a stained vacuum flask, fill it with hot water, add 15 ml/1 tbsp of bicarbonate of soda, leave it to soak overnight and rinse well.

Keep flasks fresh when not in use by popping a few lumps of sugar inside.

IF GLASSES ARE STUCK TOGETHER, STAND THE BOTTOM ONE IN HOT WATER AND POUR COLD WATER INTO THE TOP ONE – THEY WILL SEPARATE EASILY AFTER A FEW MINUTES.

FLOWERS (ARTIFICIAL)
Clean artifical flowers by shaking them in a large paper bag containing salt. Plastic flowers can be washed by dipping them in warm soapy water.

FLOWERS (CUT)
Cut flowers will stay fresher and last longer if you use soda water instead of tap water.

Always remove the lower leaves of cut flowers. They must not be submerged in the water as this harms the flowers.

An aspirin added to a vase of cut flowers gives them a new lease of life.

Short or broken stems can be lengthened by fitting them into drinking straws.

Perk up wilted flowers by plunging them first into hot water for a few minutes, then into cold water.

FLOWERS (DRIED)
To stop pieces dropping off dried flowers, spray them lightly with hairspray.

Blow dust off dried flowers using a hair dryer on a low setting.

GLASSES
Store wine glasses the right way up to avoid musty smells.

When washing glasses, put a tea towel on the draining board for the glasses to drain on.

When pouring hot liquid into a glass, put a metal spoon in first to prevent the glass from cracking.

GREENHOUSE PLANTS
When frost threatens, protect young plants by covering them in newspaper.

HANGING BASKETS
Water hanging baskets by placing ice cubes on top of the soil.

Used teabags are an excellent substitute for moss to line hanging baskets.

I LIKE MY PLANTS TO HAVE A HOLIDAY TOO

HEMLINES   If a hem mark is still visible after letting down material, sponge it with white vinegar and press it with a steam iron.

HINGES   Use cooking oil to lubricate squeaky hinges.

HOUSEPLANTS   Do not feed houseplants during the dormant winter months.

Rinse milk bottles with water to pour on houseplants as a good source of food.

Melted snow is excellent for houseplants.

If you often forget to feed your houseplants, add fertiliser pellets (available from any garden centre) to the surface of the soil, so that when you water you feed as well.

Ferns like weak tea, so bury a used tea bag in the soil.

Never use garden soil for potting or repotting houseplants, but always fresh compost.

Clean the leaves of houseplants once a month:
Tough, glossy leaves – wipe with a damp cloth.
Small leaves – spray regularly with water.
Hairy leaves – clean with a soft brush (a paint brush is ideal).

Talk to your houseplants. They really do respond to owners who stop for a chat.

When going on holiday, place all houseplants near a bowl of water and run pieces of wool from the pots to the bowl – the wool absorbs the water and slowly passes it to the plants.

WHEN DID YOU SAY THEY GET BACK?

Houseplant problems

FALLING LEAVES	Too cold Too draughty Too dry

DROOPING LEAVES	Too wet Too dry

FALLING BOTTOM LEAVES	Too dry Too warm Not enough light

YELLOW FOLIAGE	Persistently too wet May be in a draught

BROWN PATCHY LEAVES	Too sunny a position

POOR GROWTH	Not getting sufficient light

SCORCHED LOOKING LEAF TIPS	Not getting sufficient moisture

NOT FLOWERING	Not getting enough light Overfeeding

KETTLES — Descale a kettle by filling it with water and adding 30 ml/2 tbsp of vinegar. Bring to the boil, leave overnight, then empty and rinse thoroughly.

KNEELING — For all kneeling jobs, pop a cushion inside a carrier bag.

LAWNMOWER (MOTOR) — If it won't start, remove the plug and dip it in petrol. Replace and try again.

LEATHER FURNITURE — To check if it's washable, sprinkle a few drops of water on to leather that does not show. If it remains on the surface, you can wash the leather. If not, stick to dusting!

METAL SCOURING PADS — Wrap used pads in foil to prevent them from drying out and rusting.

MIRRORS — If the back of a mirror is deteriorating, try fixing a sheet of silver foil to it.

MINT — Plant mint in foil-lined holes in the garden to help to prevent it from spreading.

MOLES — Drive moles from your garden by repeatedly putting moth balls down the mole holes.

Plant 'mole spurge' (Euphorbia lathyris) at intervals around the garden.

OASIS — A potato makes a good substitute for Oasis when making a flower arrangement. Use a knitting needle to make the necessary holes.

ORANGES — Put crushed orange peel on your garden to keep cats away.

TO PREVENT PLASTER FROM CRACKING WHEN HAMMERING IN PICTURE HOOKS, STICK A PIECE OF MASKING TAPE ON FIRST

PATHS   Rid garden paths of weeds by sprinkling salt on them.

PLATES   Clean burnt plates or dishes with a damp cloth dipped in salt.

POT POURRI   Revive pot-pourri by putting it in the microwave for 30 seconds on High.

To freshen up your car, fill the ashtrays with pot-pourri.

ROSES   Banana skins dug into the beds of rose bushes provide good nutrients.

SELLOTAPE   Broad Sellotape is useful for removing fluff from clothes.

Press Sellotape into tracks of windows and doors to remove dirt, dead flies, etc.

SHOES   If leather shoes are pinching, peel a large potato and pop it into the offending shoe to soften the leather. Remove it only when it has dried out.

Pack wet shoes tightly with screwed up newspaper and allow the shoes to dry naturally.

Disguise scuffs and stains on white shoes with Tippex. Use a felt-tip pen of the appropriate colour for coloured shoes.

SHOWER SCREENS (GLASS)   Water and soap marks can be removed with a cloth dipped in white vinegar.

SILVER   Place tarnished silverware into a bowl of warm, salty water (15 ml/1 tbsp to 600 ml/1 pt), leave for 10 minutes, then rub with a soft cloth.

STRING To avoid tangles, place a ball of string into an empty baby wipes container, pulling the end through the hole in the lid.

TAPS Remove stubborn brown stains from around taps using a mixture of salt and vinegar on a soft cloth. Then clean and polish with washing-up liquid.

TEAPOTS Remove stains by leaving to soak overnight in warm water to which a denture tablet has been added. The same solution will clean stained teaspoons.

THREAD Strengthen thread for sewing buttons on jackets, etc. by first threading your needle, then running the thread over a bar of soap.

TIGHTS To stop a ladder running, spray it with hairspray, but remember to reapply it after washing. Alternatively, prevent a ladder by painting it with clear nail varnish.

TILES (VINYL) To remove a vinyl tile, cover it with silver foil and iron it with a hot iron. This softens the tile and it should then lift up easily.

FRESHEN SMELLY WELLIES AND TRAINERS BY SPRINKLING A LITTLE BICARBONATE OF SODA INSIDE

TUMBLE DRYING
If you need to dry articles quickly in a tumble dryer, put a dry towel in with them.

UNDERLAY
When laying a new carpet, put layers of newspaper on the boards for insulation.

VASES
Soak slimy flower vases with a denture tablet in the water. Then rinse and wash.

VELVET
When sewing velvet, use needles instead of pins, and tack with silk rather than cotton thread.

Velvet pile can be raised by holding it over a steaming kettle.

Never iron velvet, only ever steam it. If the article is large, try hanging over a very hot bath.

VENETIAN BLINDS
Put on cotton gloves and run the slats of a venetian blind between your fingers to clean them.

WALLPAPER
Leftover wallpaper makes good drawer liners.

WARDROBE SMELLS
An open container of bicarbonate of soda will absorb unpleasant musty smells.

WELLINGTONS
Old wellies make good holders for garden canes and sticks.

WINDOWS
Clean kitchen windows when they are steamed up. Simply wipe them with kitchen roll.

WOOL
Wind unpicked knitting wool around the ironing board and press it with a hot iron to remove kinks.

WOOLLENS
If you have run out of soap flakes, shampoo makes a good substitute.

ZIPS
Run the lead of a pencil up and down a closed zip to make it run more smoothly.

Useful tips notes

Temperatures, weights and measures

Nowadays we are expected to understand and use both imperial and metric measures, not to mention three different ways of expressing temperatures.

These conversion charts will help you with your calculations.

°C	°F	GAS
110	225	¼
120	250	½
140	275	1
150	300	2
160	325	3
180	350	4
190	375	5
200	400	6
220	425	7
230	450	8
240	475	9

OUNCES	GRAMS
1	25
2	50
3	75
4 (¼ lb)	100
5	150
6	175
7	200
8 (½ lb)	225
9	250
10	275
11	300
12 (¾ lb)	350
13	375
14	400
15	425
16 (1 lb)	450

PINTS	LITRES
¼	150 ml
½	300 ml
¾	450 ml
1	600 ml
1½	900 ml
1¾	1 litre

INCHES	CM	MM
1	2.5	25
2	5	50
4	10	100
8	20	200
12 (1 foot)	30	300
30	75	750
36 (1 yard)	90	900

INDEX